Haynes

Build your own
Website

2nd Edition

© Haynes Publishing 2009
First published 2005

Published by: Haynes Publishing
Sparkford, Yeovil, Somerset BA22 7JJ, UK
Tel: 01963 442030 Fax: 01963 440001
Int. tel: +44 1963 442030 Fax: +44 1963 440001
E-mail: sales@haynes.co.uk
Website: www.haynes.co.uk

British Library Cataloguing in Publication Data:
A catalogue record for this book is available from the British Library

ISBN 978 1 84425 658 7

Printed in Britain by J. H. Haynes & Co. Ltd., Sparkford

Haynes

Build your own
Website

2nd Edition

Gary Marshall and Kyle MacRae

Contents

Introduction

The World Wide Web has changed our lives in all kinds of ways, but if you're only reading websites then you're missing out on half the fun. These days, it couldn't be easier to publish your own pages on the web – and you can do it without spending a penny.

There are as many reasons for making websites as there are pages on the internet, ranging from the worthy to the wacky. Some people photograph their cats and publish the pictures for the world to see; others use their sites as public diaries to stay in touch with friends; families use the web to keep in touch with aunts in Australia; and people with illnesses use the web to share their experiences and provide support to others.

As making websites gets easier, more and more people are doing it. When we published the first edition of this book, Google indexed around 8 billion web pages. By 2008, that figure had risen to a whopping 25.3 billion. So why should you join in?

You're the voice

What makes the internet so amazing is that you can join in the conversation. If you think newspaper coverage of your pet subject is patchy or plain wrong, you can create your own rival publication in seconds and start putting the record straight. You could set up a site dedicated to a particular subject – politics, local events, shoes, cute things your cat does – and get chatting with like-minded souls from around the world. You could take photographs of strange places in your home town or you could build a site about your shed. The only limit is your own imagination.

Your site could be:

- An electronic magazine where you're the editor, the publisher and the star reporter
- A photo gallery that lets far-flung relatives see your snaps
- A place for you to let off steam about the things that annoy you
- A place to show off your skills, interests or strange party tricks
- A comprehensive library of information about a subject you hold dear
- A forum where like-minded souls can get together, chat and share their top tips
- An online shop selling things you've made, or things you're an expert on

...or anything else you can think of.

Options for all

There are several ways to acquire a presence on the internet and we cover three main approaches in this book:

- Designing a "traditional" page or site with WYSIWYG (what you see is what you get) software. This is as easy as writing a letter in a word processor or, perhaps more accurately, designing a leaflet with a desktop-publishing program. Grab a little free web space – we'll show you how – and you can be live and online in minutes.
- Publishing a weblog, or blog. Blogs used to be thought of as online diaries but there's much, much more to blogging than that. We'll take you through the basics and beyond.
- Building a site by hand. Yes, it sounds daunting but HTML – the language of the web – is logical and straightforward. You can easily create a page by hand using nothing more complicated, or expensive, than a free text editor program. Even if you decide to go down the WYSIWYG or blogging route, a little HTML knowledge is invaluable when it comes to understanding what's going on behind the scenes.

We also go through the processes of registering a domain name and buying web space, and we glance at the dark art of search engine optimisation and the possibility of setting up an online shop.

Designing a website and seeing it go live on the internet is a tremendously rewarding project, whether you do so just for the fun of it or with a serious purpose in mind.

A website is a living, vibrant, ever-changing thing – and maintaining your own is utterly addictive. Once you get started, there will be no stopping you.

1

PART  # So you want to build a website?

SO YOU WANT TO BUILD A WEBSITE?

Let's get started

If you can imagine it, there's a site on the internet dedicated to it. Anti-bullying? There's the Anti-Bullying Network at **www.antibullying.net**. Food? Take your pick from Delia Smith (**www.deliaonline.com**), Jamie Oliver (**www.jamieoliver.com**) or sites such as BBC Food (**www.bbc.co.uk/food**). Famous quotations? Brainy Quote (**www.brainyquote.com**). The effectiveness of different forms of medical treatment? Try **www.clinicalevidence.com**. The best articles from the world's literary journals? Arts & Letters Daily (**www.aldaily.com**). So what's your site going to be about?

Well, before you decide on the content or the look of your own site, it's a very good idea to have a look at the best and the worst sites on the World Wide Web. Some sites are spectacular, amazing electronic emporiums that make the world a better, happier or smarter place; and others are a complete waste of time and electricity.

The good: Jamie Oliver's School Dinners (www.jamieoliver.com/school-dinners)
The School Dinners pages were designed to support celebrity chef Jamie Oliver's campaign for healthier school dinners, and it was a roaring success. The site attracted 271,677 signatures for its online petition, embarrassed the government into taking action and helped thousands of parents find out more about the importance of decent school dinners.

Jamie Oliver's campaign for better school meals was a big success, and the School Dinners pages played a crucial part in putting pressure on the government.

The site itself is a great bit of web design. It's clean and uncluttered, it's easy to find your way around, and the images and colour scheme have been carefully chosen to make each page as friendly and as inviting as possible. Despite being packed with information – news, nutrition information, details of various schools' activities – it isn't intimidating; and while the site is ultimately a commercial one (there are plenty of opportunities to buy Jamie Oliver books and DVDs), it managed to achieve something worthwhile: better food for kids.

The bad: Ling's Cars (www.lingscars.com)

Ling Valentine runs a UK car rental firm and we're willing to bet she doesn't get much business from this online atrocity. It's a classic example of somebody throwing everything they can think of onto a single page, and the result is absolutely appalling. The cluttered layout makes it hard to see what matters on the website, the colours are distracting and often hard on the eyes, and the whole thing looks as if it were put together in five minutes by a toddler on a Sunny Delight binge.

It's not just bad from a design point of view – although, of course, it is bad from a design point of view. It's bad from a business point of view, too. The whole point of a business website is to say "Hi there! I'm experienced, professional and reliable, and I'm a good person to do business with." Ling's site says the absolute opposite.

Ling Valentine's site gets lots of visitors, but we suspect most of them come from appalled web designers. It's a great example of how not to build a business website.

The ugly: Time Cube (www.timecube.com)

Time Cube is quite an achievement: not only is it completely incomprehensible, but it's also horrible to look at. Text is underlined in random places before BURSTING INTO CAPITALS or appearing in retina-burning colours. If you spend more than two seconds looking at it you'll develop a migraine, so chances are you won't.

So what is Time Cube all about? We've absolutely no idea. It's utter gibberish, peppered with big words and laced with the occasional profanity. Here's one of the more accessible sentences: "Time Cube proves a 1 face god impossible, due to 4 corner face metamorphic human – baby, child and grandparent faces." If that makes sense to you, seek help immediately.

We've no idea what this chap is on about, and the headache-inducing design means we won't be hanging around to find out.

Amazon.co.uk is an amazingly successful online shop, and it owes a big part of its success to usability. It's a winning design that's been widely imitated by other online shops.

How to win friends and influence people

There are lots of really bad sites on the internet, but very few of them are intentionally bad. In many cases, the site owners forgot the Golden Rule of websites: put yourself in your visitors' shoes.

When you're putting your pages together, you need to think about usability and accessibility.

Usability is really just common sense. Is it easy to see which bits of a page are supposed to be clicked? Is the text readable? Is the layout sensible? Generally if a site looks like an explosion in a paint factory, if it's horribly cluttered and if it's impossible to work out what's going on, then the site owner hasn't thought about usability.

The best way to learn about usability is to look at a site that gets it right, such as Amazon.co.uk. It's one of the world's favourite shops, and much of its success is due to its simple, effective and very usable design. There's a big logo at the top left of the screen, and no matter where you are in the site you can click on that logo to return to the front page. Links to different bits of the site – books, DVDs, electronics and so on – are shown as tabs along the top of the screen, and it's always obvious what you need to click and what each bit of the page does.

A great deal of thought has gone into the design of Amazon.co.uk, and you'll find that most online shops look very, very similar. That's not an accident: it's a winning design, and customers now expect online shops to look and feel like Amazon. However, usability isn't limited to online shops. For example, Google is packed with powerful tools but the front page is clean, simple and effective, which means it's eminently usable. The same applies to the BBC site, or the *Guardian* newspaper site.

If a site isn't usable, it's unlikely to become successful.

Access for everyone

Usability and accessibility go together like love and marriage: if a site isn't usable, it's unlikely to be accessible either. Accessibility is incredibly important – in fact, if your site is a business one then you can be fined if it isn't accessible.

To make a site accessible, you need to think of two kinds of visitors. You need to consider the needs of people with disabilities such as partial blindness, and you need to consider the needs of people who might not have the same hardware and software as you.

The internet is a fantastic resource for people with disabilities, but thoughtless website design often puts obstacles in their way. For example, blind people can use special software called a screen reader to browse websites, but if a site designer puts all of the site's text into graphics files then the screen reader won't be able to read out those sections. There is a way around this – every well-known website design program enables you to use special tags that describe images to screen reader software – but many designers don't use those tags. Recognising this, the RNIB has put together a fantastic collection of articles about accessible websites at **www.rnib.co.uk**.

If you're running a site for business then an accessible site is a legal requirement. The Disability Discrimination Act makes it an offence for businesses to discriminate against people with disabilities, and inaccessible websites do just that. However, it's important to think about accessibility whether you're running an online shop or a daft diary. The whole point of publishing on the internet is for your site to be available to others, and an inaccessible site simply locks out a portion of your potential audience.

The wrong trousers

Imagine if Marks & Spencer wouldn't let you in unless your shoes were a very specific shade of brown, or if HMV banned any customer with black hair. Crazy? Of course it is – but a similar thing happens online every day.

Many site owners forget that not everyone in the world uses the same kit as they do. For example, you might have a PC running Internet Explorer, but some of your visitors might have an Apple Mac running the Safari browser. Until recently some big-name sites – Direct Line Insurance and Marks & Spencer, for example – wouldn't let Safari users enter their sites. Instead, a fancy bit of site design detected that they weren't using Internet Explorer and displayed a big No Entry sign. Others simply didn't work properly. If you attempted to view the Odeon Cinemas website using the Firefox or Safari browsers, you'd get a blank screen. Essentially these sites were saying to visitors, "Go away! We don't want your money!"

It's not just your web browser, though. Some people browse the web using "smart" mobile phones, or Pocket PCs, or PlayStation Portables. Some people have PCs with teeny-weeny screens, while others have monitors that are bigger than most people's TVs. Some people have one monitor on their desk, while others have two. Some people like to use high resolution displays, while others prefer nice big type. Some people browse with images turned off, while others like to see the pretty pictures. Some people have amazingly fast internet connections, while others are halfway up a hill trying to get a connection with their mobile phone.

The only thing these various people have in common is that their systems, software or setup are different to yours. The good news is that it's really easy to make sure that your site will work on any bit of kit, on any web browser and on anybody's choice of machine. We'll show you how to do just that in a later chapter.

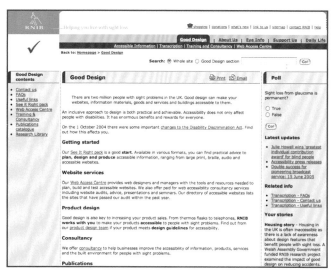

The RNIB has put together an excellent collection of resources that explains why accessibility is so important and shows you how to get it right.

Until a recent redesign, people using the Firefox web browser – currently around 20% to 30% of internet users – saw this when they visited the Odeon website. Essentially the site was saying "we don't want your money".

PART **Nuts and bolts**

Building a website is very, very easy. The World Wide Web is much simpler than you might expect, and once you understand the nuts and bolts of how websites work you'll find it easy to create a website with the "wow!" factor.

To create a website you need three things: the pages that make up the site itself, a place to put those pages, and a way to make the pages available to anyone on the internet. We'll find out how to create pages throughout this book, but before we can start creating we need to explain a few bits of jargon.

How web pages work

What makes a web page different from a normal document is the hyperlink, or link for short. Links are the bits of web pages that do something such as open another page, play a sound clip or take you to another site altogether. You'll see them on almost every page of the web. These links create a giant web of information spread across the globe, which is why the phrase World Wide Web was coined to describe it.

A web page is simply a text file that sits on a computer and contains a list of instructions. It's a bit like driving directions but instead of telling your visitors to turn left at the traffic lights, it tells your visitors' web browsing software what to show on screen, what links to include in the page and, crucially, what to do when someone clicks on one of those links.

When you look at a link, what you see on screen isn't the same thing your browser sees. For example, you might see the following text underlined in blue:

Click here to see photos of my cat!

But your browser will see something like this:

http://www.siteaboutmycats.co.uk/photos.htm

The http:// bit tells your web browser that, when you click on the link, it should load another file (http stands for HyperText Transfer Protocol, which is worth knowing if you frequent pub quizzes; otherwise you can forget about it again) and the bit after the two slashes is the actual address of that page.

Internet addresses look a bit complicated, but they're straightforward enough when you know what each bit means. In our example, the "www" means that the site is on the World Wide Web, and "siteaboutmycats.co.uk" is the name of the website. The last bit of the address is the name of the file. In this case, it's a web page called "photos.htm".

The link gives your web browser the electronic equivalent of driving directions. In our example the link says: "Go onto the internet, look on the World Wide Web for siteaboutmycats.co.uk, and then load the file called photos.htm".

Web addresses can also include folders, just like on your

Washington Post

Google offers new stock at $295
BBC News, UK - 43 minutes ago
Google says it will price its latest stock sale at $295 (£162.55) a share, more than three times the price of its initial public offering last year. ...
Calif. judge to consider throwing out **Google** suit CNET News.com
Google Wins Microsoft Case The Moscow Times
Judge's compromise ruling on **Google**-Microsoft case Financial Mirror
ZDNet UK - Wired News - all 386 related »

Pocket-lint.co.uk

Google boosts blogging
News24, South Africa - hours ago
San Francisco - A new **Google** speciality search engine sifts through the internet's millions of frequently updated personal journals, a long-anticipated ...
Google Launches Tool to Search for Blog Updates Los Angeles Times
Google Offering Raises $4.18B Red Herring
Google Launches Search Engine For Blogs InformationWeek
Washington Post - Boston Herald - all 152 related »

Google looking to get 4.4B richer
New York Daily News, NY - 1 hour ago
Google, the most-used Internet search engine, was expected to raise $4.41 billion yesterday in its first stock sale since going public, the largest such ...
Google prices stock offering at $295 per share Hindustan Times
Google stock offering at $295 per share Rediff
Google May Expand in China, Buy More Computers With Sale Funds Bloomberg
Bloomberg - Malaysia Star - all 82 related »

Google swaps hippy talk for happy talk

Web pages are full of links, usually – but not always – underlined and blue.

computer. So for example you could have addresses such as these:

http://www.siteaboutmycats.co.uk/oldstuff/photos.htm

This time, once the browser has found the "siteaboutmycats.co.uk" site, it needs to look in the folder "oldstuff" for the appropriate file. Or you might have:

http://www.siteaboutmycats.co.uk/oldstuff/archive/2004/ photos.htm

Once again the browser heads for "siteaboutmycats.co.uk" but this time the link tells it to open the "oldstuff" folder, then the "archive" folder, then the "2004" folder.

It's almost identical to the way your computer works. For example, you might save a document in your My Documents folder, and it would have the following address:

C:\My Documents\myfile.doc

Or you might have folders within the My Documents folder, such as:

C:\My Documents\house stuff\myfile.doc
C:\My Documents\daft stuff\cartoon.jpg
C:\My Documents\accounts\2005\nasty letter to the bank.doc

For reasons too dull to explain, the slashes in your web browser rise from left to right when you view files and folders, but when you're looking at folders on your computer in Windows the slashes fall from left to right.

Each file on your computer has an "address", just like every page on the internet.

So, we know how web addresses work – but you can't have an address if your pages aren't on the internet in the first place. To do that, we'll need to explore the world of web space.

Are you being served?

Every website needs to be stored on something called a web server, which is a fancy way of saying "computer". A web server is simply a computer with a bit of hard disk space and a permanent internet connection, and it's configured in such a way that it can dish out web pages whenever your visitors request them.

Although it's possible to run your own web server, it's a much better idea to let someone else do it on your behalf. That means you don't need to worry about setting up the server, mucking around with advanced configuration options and ensuring that it has a permanent internet connection.

Firms who provide space for web pages are known as hosting firms, because they host your website on your behalf. There are hundreds of such firms to choose from, and they offer a huge range of packages ranging from free and easy services for internet beginners to massive systems for giant online shops.

Firms such as Tripod can give you everything you need to publish your website, and their most basic package is free of charge.

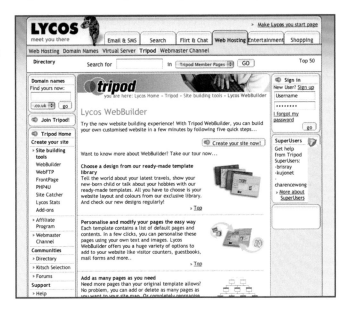

To pay or not to pay

Web hosting comes in two flavours: free hosting, which enables you to publish a site without paying a penny, and paid hosting, which costs money.

Free hosting is available from firms such as Tripod (**www.tripod.co.uk**) and is designed to be beginner-friendly. You'll get enough space for a decent collection of pages, a few tools to help you improve your site such as free guestbook software, free images or other goodies, and signing up only takes a few seconds. However, there is a trade-off. Most such services will add advertising banners or pop-up windows to your pages, and you'll find that few free hosts will let you store video clips, music files or other hefty downloads.

Paid hosting costs money, but it's much more flexible. Firms such as Pipex (**www.pipex.net**) and 1&1 (**www.oneandone.co.uk**) offer packages starting at just £4.99 per month, and they won't add any advertising to your site. Depending on the specific package you choose you'll usually be able to store video clips, music files and other big files, and you'll get much more space and much more scope than with a free host.

So which should you choose? The table below shows the key differences between a typical free hosting service and one that costs money.

Before you make the decision, though, it's a very good idea to see if your Internet Service Provider gives you any web space as part of your internet connection package. Many ISPs do, and it's a good compromise between the two kinds of hosting: the space comes free with your internet service but it won't spoil your pages by plastering adverts all over the place.

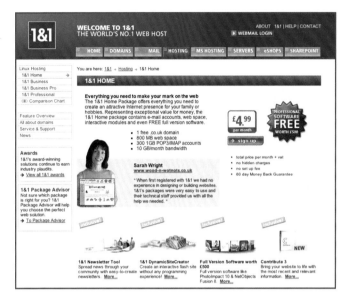

Paid-for web hosting is much more flexible than free hosting and prices aren't too scary: 1&1's home package starts at £4.99 per month.

	Typical free host	Typical paid host
How much will I pay?	Nothing	From £4.99 per month
Will the firm add adverts?	Yes	No
How much web space will I get?	Not much	Lots
Can I get more space if I need it?	For a fee	For a fee
Can I use photos?	Yes	Yes
Can I use video?	Probably not	Yes
Can I use sound files?	Probably not	Yes
Is it easy to set up?	Very	Fairly
What happens if I get too many visitors?	Site may be temporarily unavailable	You may incur extra charges,but only after attracting serious visitor numbers
Can I sell ad space on my site?	Depends on the hosting firm	Yes
Can I run an online shop?	Not usually	Yes
Can I install extra features?	Only host-approved ones	Yes, anything you like
Will I get technical support?	Not usually	Yes
Will the firm take backups of my site?	Not usually	Yes
Who is it best for?	Beginners, very simple sites	Everyone

What's in a name?

No matter what kind of hosting you go for, the address of your website is likely to be rather complicated. In most cases, you'll end up with something like this:

www.hostingfirm.com/hosting/users/g535433/index.html

You can change this by getting your own domain name. Domain names are the addresses of internet sites such as Amazon.co.uk, Google.com, BBC.co.uk and so on, and you can pick up one of your very own for around £3 from a site such as 123Reg (**www.123reg.co.uk**). Once you've bought the name, it's yours for two years and you can point it to your website through the 123Reg control panel. That means your site can have a snappier name such as "mygreatsite.co.uk" instead of the random-looking address you get with your web space.

There are several good reasons for buying a domain name. First, it's easier to remember. Secondly, it makes your site more search-friendly. Search engines give weight to a site's domain name, so if two sites have identical content but one is called **interestingthings.com** and the other is **hostingfirm.com/space/2005/users/jim/home**, then the snappier name will appear higher in search results for the phrase "interesting things".

The third reason to get a domain name is that it's portable, so if you're currently using a free web host and decide to move to paid hosting, you can simply point the domain name to your site's new location. Similarly if you decide that your current paid host isn't up to the job and you want to move to a competitor, you can do so without any disruption whatsoever.

Before you buy a domain name it's worth looking at the different options. While **.com** domains are the most desirable, they cost £30+ to register; **.org.uk** domains should only be used by non-profit organisations; **.ltd.uk** domains are for UK Limited Companies; and gimmicky domains such as **.me** and **.biz** are rather naff. The best all-rounder is the **.co.uk** domain, which is very popular and very cheap.

Once you've chosen the kind of domain name you want, you also need to choose the name itself. This can be a bit of a minefield, for two reasons: many of the obvious names have already been sold, and you also need to make sure you don't upset anyone with more money than you. For example, "markzandspencer.co.uk" might still be available to buy, but if you use it you can expect an unfriendly letter from Marks & Spencer's crack legal team. If any firm thinks you're trying to attract visitors that are rightfully theirs, expect legal hot water.

Don't bother with generic terms such as "food", "shopping", "news", "computers" and so on: you can be sure they've been snapped up already (for instance, **www.food.co.uk** takes you to a shopping directory). Most common surnames have been taken, as have common first name/surname combinations. That's why there are so many internet companies with weird names: they racked their brains until they came up with a domain name that was available, and when they came up with one they named the company after it. You might find that you need to do a bit of lateral thinking to come up with a suitably snappy domain name that hasn't already been snapped up by somebody else.

You can buy a snappy domain name such as "mygreatsite.co.uk" for around £3 per year.

Buying a domain name and hosting

Now that we've discovered the importance of domain names and web space, the next step is to buy them both. If you've already got free web space from your ISP or from a free hosting provider, then you might want to experiment with that before spending any money. However, if you want your site to look the business then a decent domain name and professional, ad-free web space will be a big help.

Web hosting is fiercely competitive, so it pays to shop around. At the time of writing, 123reg (**www.123reg.co.uk**) was offering one of the best deals around, with an entry-level hosting package for just £1.85 per month. Click on the Web Hosting tab to find out what you get for your cash.

The package we're interested in is the first one, called Starter. This gives you 100MB of web space, which is more than adequate for a reasonable-sized website, and you also get full FTP access, webmail and some useful site statistics that help you see who's visiting your site, how they got there and where they came from.

Before you buy your hosting, though, you need a domain name. If you've shopped with 123reg before, login; if you haven't, you'll need to register. Once you've done that, click on Register and enter the domain name you'd like to use. Clicking on the Search button will show you whether that name is available in various flavours including .co.uk, .com and so on.

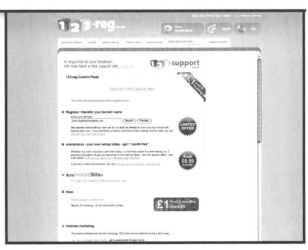

4

Although there are lots of different suffixes, there's no point in registering them all: a .co.uk address is perfect for the majority of British sites. Select the domain you'd like to register and add it to your shopping basket.

5

If you wish, you can register other domains at the same time. For now, though, we'll stick with one. If you've chosen a domain by mistake, you can get rid of it by clicking on the cross icon next to its name. Once you've got the domain you want in your shopping basket, click on "Ok, let's continue" to go to the next step.

6

They're helpful people at 123-reg so, when you order your domain name, the site asks whether you want to order extras. In this case we do, because we want to buy some web space. Scroll down, click on "show web hosting" and choose the Starter package. Click on "add to basket".

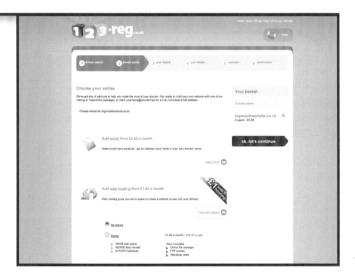

You'll notice that the prices that appear in your basket aren't as low as you might expect. That's because of three things: when you buy a .co.uk domain, it's for a period of two years; hosting is billed annually, not monthly; and when you choose a hosting package, there's a setup fee (in this case, £9.99). There's not much you can do about this, so click on "ok, let's continue".

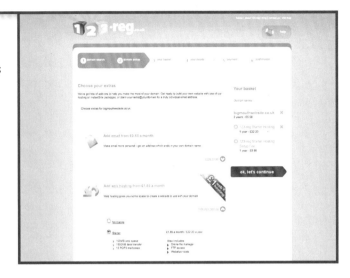

The website now shows your shopping basket again. Double-check you've entered the correct domain name and the hosting package you want, and then click on the "ok, let's sign in" button to continue.

When you buy a domain name, you need to provide a name, address and contact details. If you're an individual rather than a company or other organisation you can prevent this information from being made publicly available – although this option only applies to .uk domain names. Check the box if you'd rather keep your details private. Once you've done this, click on "Continue to payment" and enter your card details.

The index page

Your new domain name and hosting should be available immediately, but when you type your brand new address into your browser's address bar you'll notice something weird: instead of a blank page, which is what you'd expect, you get the front page of the 123reg website. That's because browsers expect to find a file called index.html or index.htm on a website, and we haven't created that file yet. Instead of showing your visitors an error when index.html isn't present, hosting firms such as 123reg redirect visitors to their front page.

Don't worry, your site won't be advertising a hosting firm for long – in the next section we'll start to put our first site together.

We have lift-off!

You've sorted out your hosting firm and you've bought a suitably snappy domain name. The final step is to create your web pages and stick them on your hosting firm's server. Once they're there, they'll be available to the entire internet.

As we'll discover in the following chapters, creating web pages is just as easy as writing a letter in a word processor or creating a new message in an email program. But how do you get the pages onto the internet when you've finished making them? The answer is FTP.

FTP is short for File Transfer Protocol and it's a way for computers to communicate with web servers. To use it you'll need a program called an FTP client, or you can use the online File Manager tools provided by many hosting firms. It sounds complicated but it's really straightforward: it's just a matter of logging in with the correct user name and password (the FTP system will be password protected to make sure that only you can update your site) and then dragging the files from your computer to the web server. And that's it!

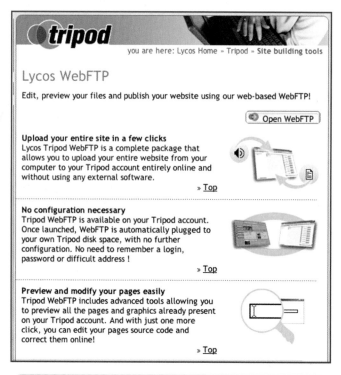

Most hosting firms provide FTP software that runs in your web browser and makes it easy to upload pages to the internet.

Top tip

Remember that when you buy a domain name, it's for a fixed period (usually two years) and you'll need to renew it when the expiry date approaches. The firm from which you bought your domain name will usually give you lots of notice, but if they don't or you forget to do anything then you might find that your chosen name has been snapped up by someone else – a competitor, perhaps, or someone doing something you don't approve of. That could be embarrassing if your Gran decides to visit your website and discovers it's been replaced with something filthy.

PART

Designing a traditional site

In the very early days of the internet, you needed to know a special language to create web pages. This language was called HTML (HyperText Markup Language) and looked something like this:

```
<b>This text would appear in bold</b>
<i>This text would appear in italics</i>
```

It's actually very similar to the way word-processing software used to work, although of course these days you'd just click the Bold button to make your text bold. The good news is that the same thing has happened in website design, and there are plenty of programs that look and work pretty much like a word-processing program or a drawing program but which create the HTML pages that make up your site. Such programs are called WYSIWYG (pronounced "wizzywig"), which is short for What You See Is What You Get.

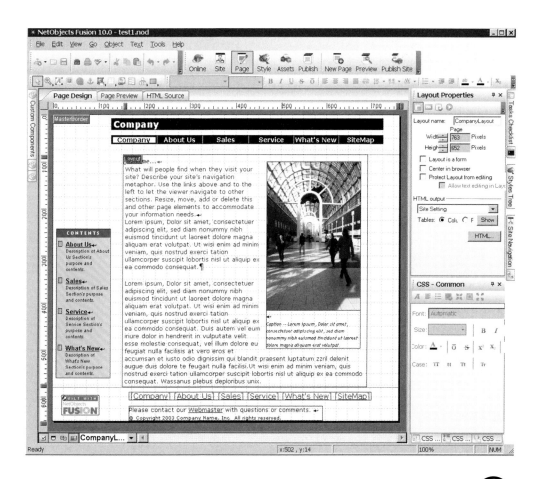

Web design programs

There are hundreds of web design programs on the market, and they're designed to help you make anything from a simple web page to an online shop – but they do things in very different ways. Here are some of the better-known examples.

Microsoft Expression Web

www.microsoft.com
£60 (student version); £274 (full version)
Microsoft's replacement for the ageing FrontPage web design program is very powerful, but it's also very pricey unless you qualify for the student version. We think it's a little too complicated for beginners and hobbyists but if you need to build a big, complicated site it's certainly worth the money.

Serif WebPlus SE

www.freeserifsoftware.com
Free
Serif have spent years making easy to use desktop publishing software and WebPlus is essentially the same software but for web pages. It's not the most powerful package you can get, but you can't argue with a price tag of zero. For quick and simple site building, it's hard to beat.

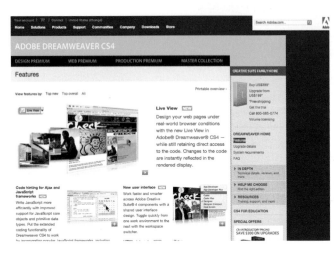

Adobe Dreamweaver

www.adobe.com
£89 (student version); £339 (full version)
Visit any professional web design agency and you'll almost certainly see Dreamweaver on their machines –with good reason: it's an exceptionally good program. As with Expression Web, it's pricey unless you get a student discount and it's definitely overkill for people building their first few sites.

Apple iWeb

www.apple.com/uk/ilife
Free (with new Macs); £55
Everyone who buys a new Apple Mac gets iWeb, which is part of the iLife suite of video and photography tools. It's designed to work closely with iPhoto and other Apple applications and, in typical Mac style, the results are gorgeous. If you're a Mac user, you should definitely consider iWeb before spending any money on a more heavyweight package, such as Dreamweaver.

NetObjects Fusion Essentials

www.netobjects.com
Free
Essentials is a stripped-down version of the well-regarded Fusion program, which is powerful enough to build an entire online shop. While the free version isn't quite so muscular, it's still a surprisingly good program that's easy to use without being too simple. Of the various free web design programs, Fusion Essentials is our favourite – which is why we'll be using it in our very first tutorial.

Other options

It's possible to build a website without using any software at all – although the tools available depend very much on the sites you visit or the hosting firm you use. For example, customers of the hosting firm 1&1 get a free website builder that runs in their web browsers; while it's very basic, it's fine if you just want to bash out a few pages. Alternatively, you could go to Google Sites (formerly known as Page Creator), **sites.google.com**, which does much the same thing for free.

If you're only planning to do one thing – such as write a weblog, share photos online or upload the odd video – then you might find that free online services do everything you need. As we'll discover in Part 3, you can create a blog without using any software at all, and it's easy to bring in photos and videos from other sites – so you can store your photos on Flickr.com, upload videos to YouTube.com and then bring them all together on your website or on Blogger.com.

If you're in a hurry to get your words on the internet then a free service such as Google Page Creator is certainly the fastest way to go, but if you want to make a site that really sings, then it's much better to use a dedicated web design program. There are a few reasons for this. First of all, the software is easy to use so it won't take long to get the hang of things. Secondly, you're not limited to the handful of designs you'll find on free, web-based services, and you can still take advantage of services such as YouTube and Flickr. And most importantly of all, as you get more confident a dedicated web design program can keep up with you when you start to spread your wings.

In the workshop that follows, we'll show you everything you need to get your very first pages on the World Wide Web.

Sites such as **www.Bravenet.com** offer lots of free add-ons for your site, but use them judiciously or you'll ruin your design.

PART  Building a basic web page

In this workshop, we'll put together a straightforward web page and make it available on the internet. To do this, we'll use the free Fusion Essentials program and some free web space from Tripod. As you'll discover, putting your words on the web couldn't be easier.

Before you start building a web page, it's a very good idea to collate the bits and bobs you plan to use – in this example, we've created a new folder containing some photographs we'd like to include in our web page. Having everything you need in one place saves a great deal of time later on.

Download NetObjects Fusion Essentials from **www.netobjects.com** *and install it. You'll need to provide a valid email address on this registration screen: NetObjects uses this to email the serial number for your software. The email usually arrives in your inbox within a few seconds. Once you've entered the serial number, you can finish installing the software.*

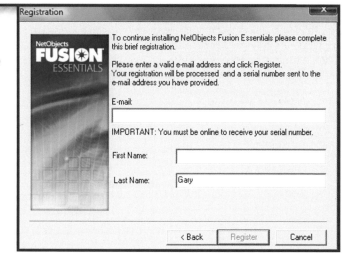

3

Launch the program and you should see the screen here, which is rather keen on selling you a few upgrades. Ignore the bumph for now and click on File > New Site > Using Site Wizard to begin creating your very first website.

4

The Site Wizard will now appear. Skip the first page and you'll be given the choice of a business site or a personal one. We'll use the personal option, which automatically creates four pages: About Me, Hobbies, Favourites and Photo Gallery.

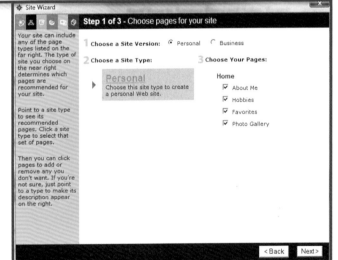

5

The Site Wizard will now ask you to choose a visual style for your site. To pick a design, click on the options in the first form field; to change the colours, use the drop-down box under the "Choose a color" section. The preview in the middle of the window will automatically update to display your choices.

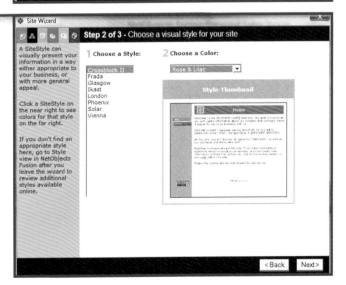

6

The program will now ask you to create a profile containing your contact details. We wouldn't bother, as it's rarely a good idea to put such information on the internet where anybody can see it. Click Cancel to continue.

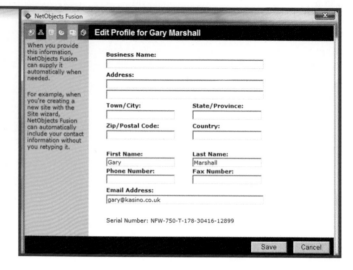

7

Click on Finish and Fusion Essentials will ask where it should save your site files. This is where the folder we created earlier comes in handy, because we'll put our files in that. Give your site a name – it doesn't matter what you call it – and click on Save.

8

Fusion Essentials will now create your website and display the site structure, as shown here. As you can see there are five pages: a home page, a hobbies page, a favourites page and two photos pages. Double-click on Home to see it.

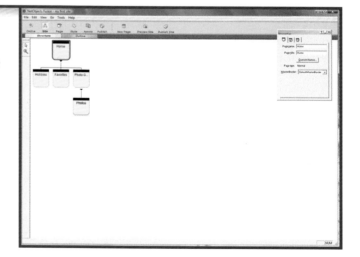

You should now see something that looks like a desktop publishing package – and in fact, it works in much the same way. At first, your page will seem rather short. To fix that, grab the ruler (immediately to the left of the page) and drag it downwards. Your page should automatically resize.

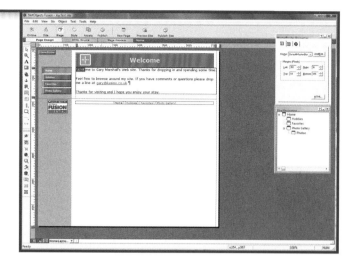

That's better. Time to make things more interesting: if you click on any part of the page you can move it by dragging and dropping. Try moving the text links (the box with "[home] [hobbies]", and so on) to the bottom of your page, making the text box thinner and longer and replacing the text in the box with something better.

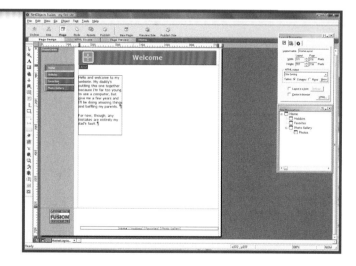

We're getting there, but the page would look a lot better with a picture. To add one, click on the Picture icon – it's the fourth icon in the toolbar at the very left-hand side of the screen – and use it to draw a box where you'd like your photo to go. The program will then ask you to choose a photo. Aren't you glad you sorted them out earlier?

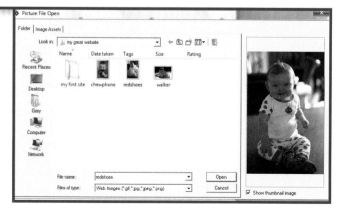

Your photo will now appear on your page, and you can resize it or move it like any other object. Click on the Page Preview tab at the top of the window to see exactly how your page will appear in a web browser, and click on Page Design to go back to the design screen. If you're curious about the HTML code that makes the page work, you can click on HTML Source to see it.

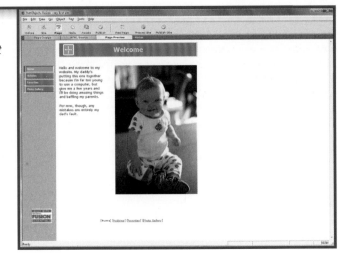

Once you're happy with your home page, it's time to turn your attention to the rest of your site. Click on the Site icon at the top of the screen to return to the Site Structure view, which shows all the pages in your site. Now, double-click on the Photos page icon.

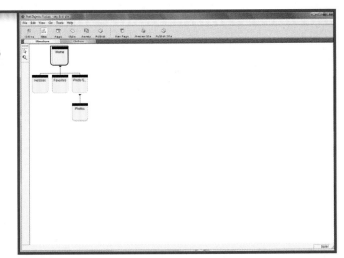

As you can see, the program has already used a photo – and of course, we want to use our own. To do this, double-click on the photo to bring up the Photo Gallery Editor. This enables you to replace the standard photos with your own pictures.

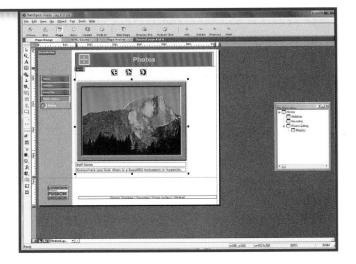

To remove the standard images, click on Delete All. Now use the Add button to select your own photos one at a time. Your pictures will appear in the left-hand section of the screen, and you can add titles and captions in the right-hand section of the screen. Click on Done when you've finished.

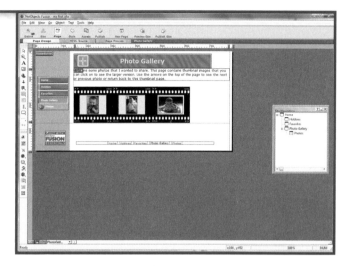

You'll now be taken to the photos page, but as you can see the original photos have been replaced with yours. If you click on Photo Gallery in the site navigation panel at the right of the screen, you'll see that your photos have also been used in the Photo Gallery page – which is exactly what we want.

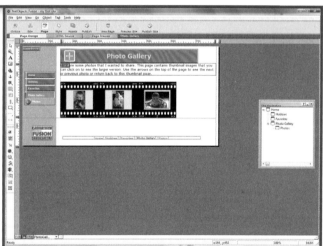

Although you can use Fusion Essentials' Page Preview button to see what individual pages look like, you can't test your entire site that way. Instead, click on Preview Site in the toolbar. This creates a temporary copy of your site on your hard disk and opens it in your web browser, so you can see exactly how it will look when you publish it online.

When you're previewing your site in your web browser, all the links work – so you can click on Photo Gallery and then on an individual photo to see it. If something doesn't look quite right then just switch back to Fusion Essentials and edit it.

We're not too happy with the way our photos page appears, so we'll move the navigation buttons. You can select multiple objects at once by dragging the mouse over them, which we've done here. Everything can be moved by dragging and dropping.

Once you're happy with your changes, click on Preview Site again – you can't just refresh the web browser, because the files it's using won't be updated until Fusion Essentials has re-exported them. It's worth experimenting with different layout ideas and tweaking the settings in the Photo Gallery editor until you're happy with the finished pages.

Creating and using your own header image

One of the things we hate about free programs is that the default templates are rather dull. No problem: simply download the free Paint.net program (**www.getpaint.net**) and you can create your own. Install the program and create a new image.

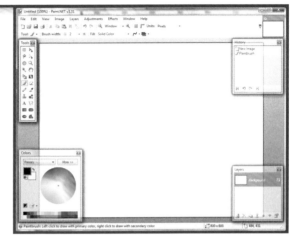

Click on Image > Canvas Size and set the width to 400 pixels and the height to 100 pixels. This is a good size for a header image. You can now use the text and shape tools to draw anything you like, although for this image we'll keep it simple with a bit of coloured text.

Click on File > Save As and give your image a name. Change the file type to JPEG (the default is PNG), and make sure you save the image in the same folder as your other website images. Once you've done this, close Paint.net and return to Fusion Essentials.

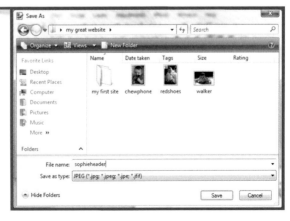

④

To change our header image, we need to change the site style. To do this, click on the Style icon in the toolbar and you'll see a screen showing all the different images in the standard template. To change the banner image, double-click on it.

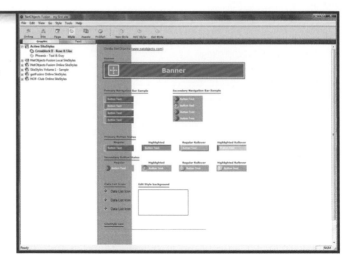

⑤

You'll now see a screen telling you that you can't edit the style and asking if you want to create a new one based on it. Say yes and give the new style a meaningful name (in the list at the left of the screen). This time, if you double-click on the banner image you'll be able to change it.

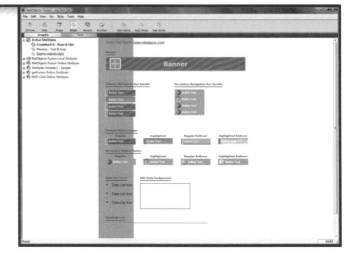

⑥

Navigate to the folder where you keep all your images and select the new header design you created in Paint.net. A preview will appear in the right of the window so you can see what you've selected. Click on Open when you've found the right one.

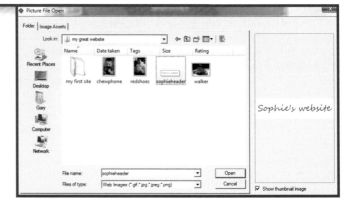

Now, click on the Set Style button at the top of the screen. This will make your edited style apply to your whole website, so if everything is working properly your new header should appear on all of the pages. To test this, click on Page and then double-click on one of your pages.

We're nearly there: the image is in the right place, but there's text over it. To get rid of the text, right-click over it and choose Object Properties. The properties palette should now pop up and you can delete the text from the "Banner" field. You'll need to do this for each page.

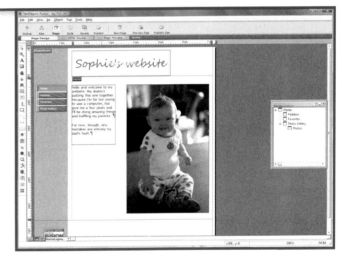

Let's see how that looks. Click on Preview Site and your web browser will now open, and your new image should be at the top of every page. It's worth double-checking each page to make sure there isn't any text sitting on top of the header image – it's easy to miss! Close the browser, return to Fusion Essentials and click on File > Save Site when you're finished.

PART 1

Getting online with free web space

Signing up for free web space is simple, if a little time-consuming. Go to **www.tripod.co.uk** and then click on Join Tripod. This will take you to a page with a prominent "create your free account now!" link. If you click on this link you'll have to wade through the site terms and conditions, and you'll have to provide some basic details such as your name and address. You'll also need to choose a user name and password. Watch out for the small print: if you don't specify otherwise by ticking the appropriate boxes, Tripod will pass your details on to other firms so they can annoy you with ads (or as Tripod puts it, send you "exciting and useful information from Lycos Partners").

Once you've finished the sign-up procedure, Tripod will send you an email containing a website link. You need to click on this link to complete the registration process.

When you receive your email from Tripod, clicking on the included link will take you to the registration confirmation page. This will ask you to choose an FTP password. It's important that you take a note of whatever password you choose, as you'll use it whenever you upload pages to your Tripod web space.

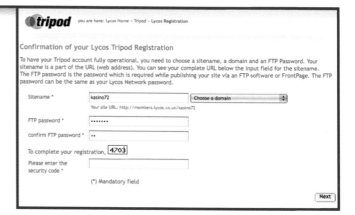

In Fusion Essentials, click on Publish > Publish Settings. Now, we need to create a new profile to store our website data. Click on New Profile, ensure the Remote button is checked and then click on OK.

3

Enter the details from your Tripod email (if the mail didn't arrive, log in at **www.tripod.lycos.co.uk** *and select My Account > Settings to get the details) as follows:*

FTP host: ftp.members.lycos.co.uk
User name: your Tripod username
Password: the password you selected when you signed up

Click on OK and then click on Publish Site.

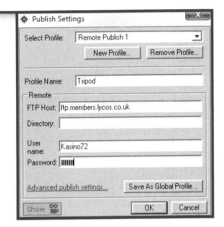

4

The program will now ask you where to publish your files, so make sure it's set to the Tripod profile that you've just created. Click on Publish to continue.

5

Once the upload has finished, your site should be online at **http://members.tripod.co.uk/username** *(where "username" is the user name you chose when you signed up with Tripod). You'll see that in addition to your design, there are a lot of ads; that's the price you pay for free web hosting.*

PART 2

Building bigger sites

PART **2**

Smart planning

As we've discovered, it's easy to put together a few pages and put them on the web. However, when you're building bigger sites, it's a very good idea to do some planning before you reach for your web design program. A little bit of forward thinking can save you a great deal of time and effort, and it can prevent you having to rebuild an entire site from scratch later on.

The most important weapon in any web designer's arsenal isn't a fast computer or a powerful program: it's a bit of paper and a pencil. Use them to create an outline of your site that details the pages your site will include, and what you'll call them. If you're the artistic type you can also sketch out a rough design for your site, which will save you a bit of time when it comes to putting the actual pages together.

Thinking ahead

To create your site outline, you need to know what your site is going to do – which means knowing who your audience will be. For example, if you're building a site to show off your photography skills, then your visitors will want to see your pictures. A sensible site structure might look a bit like this:

- Home page
- About me page
- Portrait photography
- Landscape photography
- Arty photography

That's a fairly simple example, but you could expand on it like this:

- Home page
- About me page
- Portrait photography
    Children
    Families
    Celebrities
- Landscape photography
    UK
    Europe
    USA
- Arty photography

What's good about this way of doing things is that you can see at a glance what pages you need and what links you'll need to have on your pages. So for example, our photographer might need the following pages:

File name	Purpose of page
Index.html	Home page
About.html	About Me page
Portrait.html	Portrait photography: main page
Kidportraits.html	Portraits: children
Familyportraits.html	Portraits: family
Celebportraits.html	Portraits: celebrities
Landscape.html	Landscape photography: main page
UKland.html	Landscapes: UK
Euroland.html	Landscapes: Europe
USAland.html	Landscapes: USA

As you can see, by scribbling a rough site structure on a bit of paper our photographer can see that he or she needs to create ten distinct web pages.

A rough sketch on paper is the essential first step en route to the web.

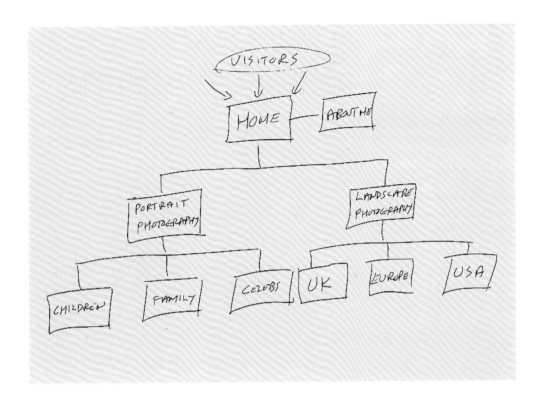

Oh, goodies

There are stacks of sites that offer all kinds of add-ons for your site, and you'll find that many web design programs also include things called "widgets", "smart objects" or something similar. Typically these are little bits of code that you can add to your site. Examples include:

- Discussion forums
- Guest books
- Calendars
- Little buttons saying "made with…"
- Visitor statistics
- Special effects

It's tempting to add such items to your site, but it's important to choose any goodies carefully. In many cases add-ons can make your site look worse rather than better, so for example if you have a discussion board that nobody uses, visitors will get a much worse impression of your site than if you didn't have a discussion forum at all.

The same applies to many other add-ons. Calendars are often useless, little buttons saying "I made this site with…" are rather naff, and special effects are almost always a bad idea. For example, you can get a special effect that takes a picture and adds what looks like a moving, watery reflection immediately below it, but the code to make this happen takes forever to download and the effect itself has long since fallen out of fashion.

The golden rule of goodies is "if in doubt, leave it out".

eFreeGuestbooks Demo Book

Please do not post support questions in this book, we do not respond to support questions posted here

Sign eFreeGuestbooks Demo Book   Return to eFreeGuestbooks

Entry #: 991
Name: ssssssssssss
Email: Protected
Site Rating: 10
Comments: ©
xxxxxxxxxxxxxxxxxxxxxxxxxxxxxxxxxxxxxxxxxxxxxxxxxxxxxxxxxxxxxxxxxxxxxxxxxxxxxxxxxxxxxxxxxxxxxxxxxxxxxxxxxXXXXXXXXX

Entry #: 990
Name: dude
Site Rating: 10
Comments: testing . . .

Entry #: 989
Private Entry ⌂

Entry #: 988
Name: John
Web Site: Silvertrain

Free add-ons such as guestbooks may be tempting, but as you can see they often look appalling.

Everyone's a winner

There's no big secret to building a successful site. All you need to know are two very straightforward rules: the KISS rule and the two-click rule.

KISS stands for "keep it simple and straightforward" and it's what differentiates good sites from bad ones. Sites that make visitors endure a pointless animation before taking them to the home page have forgotten the KISS rule, and their visitors are likely to head off for another site long before the animation has finished loading.

With the internet, less is more: a few well-chosen images will have more impact on a page than hundreds of flashing buttons, and a few paragraphs of simple, well-written text will be easier to read and more attractive to the eye than endless blocks of tiny type.

The two-click rule is particularly important if you're trying to sell things, but it applies to any kind of site. It's a simple rule that makes a big difference, and it says:

"Visitors should be able to find what they're looking for with just two mouse clicks."

In the case of our photographer's site, that means people should be able to find the photos they want to see with two mouse clicks. Does our rough site structure follow that rule? It does: to get to portraits of children, for example, visitors need only click the "children" link and then the photo they want to see.

The two-click rule works just as well on giant sites as it does on small ones. If you're buying a new TV online, you'll find that even the biggest electrical sites enable you to find TVs by clicking Audio-Visual and then Televisions.

With really big sites, the two-click rule usually means that visitors should be able to find the appropriate product category in two clicks, rather than a specific product. In our TV example above, two clicks does indeed take you to the TV section of an electrical site, but instead of seeing the entire range of televisions – which could run to hundreds of different products – you'll then see links for different kinds of TVs: portable TVs, standard TVs, widescreen TVs, LCD TVs, Plasma TVs, projector TVs and so on. Using categories like this is the best way to combine the two-click rule with the KISS rule.

If you're planning to include lots and lots of content in your site, spend a bit of time browsing similar sites to get an idea of how they organise their pages. Such browsing will give you a really good idea of how to organise your own site, which will save you a lot of time and an awful lot of effort.

Sites such as **www.comet.co.uk** follow the two-click rule. For example, if you want to buy a TV, click on Home Entertainment and then on Plasma & LCD TVs.

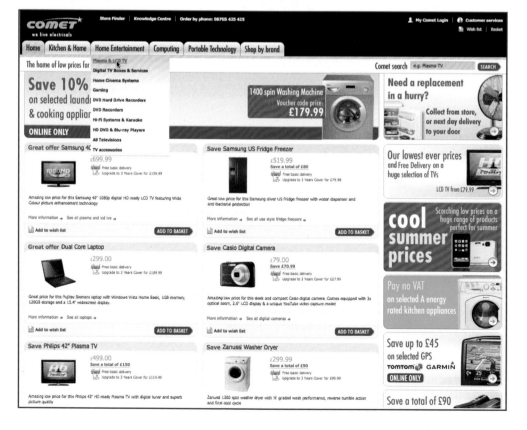

FreeFoto.com is a great source of images that you can use in your site, and if it's a non-profit site you can use the images free of charge.

Copyrights and wrongs

A picture's worth a thousand words, but what if you don't have any pictures? If you're not a photographer, how do you get some images for your site?

Unfortunately, getting pictures for your website isn't as simple as doing a Google Image Search (**http://images.google.com**), finding what you want and then adding it to your site. Most images you'll see online are protected by copyright, which means that only the owner of those images has the right to make copies of them. Infringing copyright is illegal, and if you're caught doing it you'll be forced to remove the offending images at best, or sued silly at worst.

Don't despair, though, because there are lots of places where you can get free, high-quality images legally. One of our favourites is FreeFoto (**www.freefoto.com**), which at the time of writing boasts 74,630 images in 2,577 categories. There are pictures of UK landmarks, of spectacular weather, of animals... if you can imagine it, FreeFoto probably has a photo of it.

High quality photographs for free – surely there's a catch? There is, but it's not a scary one. You're allowed to use FreeFoto's images only for private, non-commercial use, so if you're making money from your site then you'll have to pay for your pictures. However, for home or charity sites, you can use as many FreeFoto images as you like provided that you credit the site on your home page and provide a link back to the FreeFoto site.

Another good source of content is the Creative Commons site at **http://creativecommons.org**. Here you'll find all kinds of things – photos, music and even movies – put together by people who want to share their work with others. Each image (or music file, or movie) will come with a Creative Commons licence that tells you exactly what you can and cannot do with it, so for example you'll find lots of images that you can use on your own site provided you don't modify the images or try to pass them off as your own work.

Writing for the web

It's amazing how many people create beautiful-looking websites and then ruin them with giant blocks of tiny, hard-to-read text. For most sites the text is the important bit, so it's important to get it right.

Reading text on a computer screen is very different from reading printed text. While a newspaper will happily put 1,000 words of densely packed type on a single page – and newspaper buyers will happily read it – the same text on a web page would look horrible and intimidating. Internet readers tend to have shorter attention spans than newspaper readers, too, so too much text is a no–no.

There are two things to consider when you're writing text for the web: what you're saying, and how it looks. Here are our top tips:

Keep it short

Simple, punchy sentences will be much more effective than really long sentences, which use lots of interruptions (some with commas, some with brackets and some – or even many – with dashes) and tend to drag on a lot; in many cases you could chop 75% of the sentence out and still make sense.

Jargon is junk

This is a particular peril in the world of business websites, where far too many firms call a spade a metallic gardening implement and sandwich firms "provide portable meal solutions". Call a spade a spade!

Break it up

This:

> Too busy to shop? We can help. Tell us what you want and we'll:
>
> - Find the perfect product
> - Get it at the best possible price
> - Deliver it to your door
>
> 100% Safe Shopping guarantee – click here to find out more!

Is better than this:

> Too busy to shop? We can help. Tell us what you want and we'll find the perfect product, get it at the best possible price and deliver it to your door. Our Safe Shopping Guarantee means you can shop with confidence; click here to find out more.

Web users are a bit like magpies: they look at the shiny things first. On a web page that means your visitors' eyes will be attracted to headlines, to bullet points and to anything highlighted rather than to solid blocks of text.

Short paragraphs with text broken by clear lines and if necessary spread over two or more pages makes reading on the web a more pleasurable experience.

A few simple things can make a big difference. For example, a single blank line between paragraphs makes text feel a lot less cluttered, and a half-dozen short paragraphs looks much friendlier than two very long ones. If you're publishing really long bits of text, such as essays, articles or long rants about the evils of traffic wardens, then consider splitting the text over a few pages. You'll find that many newspaper sites do this.

Choose your colours
Most of the things we read tend to use dark text on a light background, and with good reason: it's easy on the eyes. Only use unusual colour combinations if you're absolutely sure what you're doing, or you could end up with text that looks pretty from a distance but which makes your visitors' eyes bleed when they actually try to read it.

Fix your fonts
The KISS rule applies to your fonts as well as the overall design of your site. We'd recommend sticking to a maximum of two different fonts: one for headlines, and one for the main text.

Some fonts work better online than others. For example, clean fonts such as Arial, Verdana and Georgia were designed for on-screen viewing and unsurprisingly work very well. Other fonts – particularly gimmicky ones – are hard to read, and may not be present on your visitors' computers. If in doubt, go with the tried and tested typefaces.

Think about search engines
Most search engines analyse the content of pages, so it's a good idea to think of the search terms people might use to find sites like yours. For example, if you're a portrait photographer then you'd expect people to search for sites like yours by using terms such as "portrait photographer London", "family photographs" or something similar. Using these terms in your site's body text will improve your site's visibility in search engine results.

Newspaper sites use black text on white backgrounds because it's very easy to read. Avoid dark backgrounds and light coloured text.

Getting on Google

If the search engine Google doesn't know about your site, it might as well not exist. Google will normally find your site without any intervention from you, but there are a few tricks you can use to make your site more Google-friendly.

We've already mentioned that you should include suitable search terms in your pages' text, but you should also try the following:

Use an appropriate title

Google (and other search engines) will display your page title in their search results, so it's a good idea to give each page a descriptive title. For example, "My first site" won't be as effective as "pictures of my black Labrador". Use a different title for each page, so for example in the case of our photographer, one page might be titled "Joe Bloggs: Portrait photography" and another might be "Joe Bloggs: Landscape photography."

Enter a description

Most web design programs enable you to insert a description into your page, usually in the Page Properties section. This doesn't appear anywhere on your site, but it is visible to search engines and it's what appears immediately below your page title in search results. Use this section to describe who you are or what your site is.

For example, our photographer might write: "Joe Bloggs is a portrait and landscape photographer based in London, specialising in pictures of children and families".

Get linked

The more popular a site, the more important Google thinks it is and the higher it will appear in search engine results. One way in which Google judges popularity is by looking at the sites that link to a particular page, so if you can persuade people to link to you then your site will rise up the search engine rankings.

You can find out more about Google site listings at **www.google.co.uk/intl/en/webmasters/**, which is an excellent collection of how-to articles.

Google has an extensive help section that tells you everything you need to know about getting your site listed in its giant database – and what dirty tricks will get your site blacklisted.

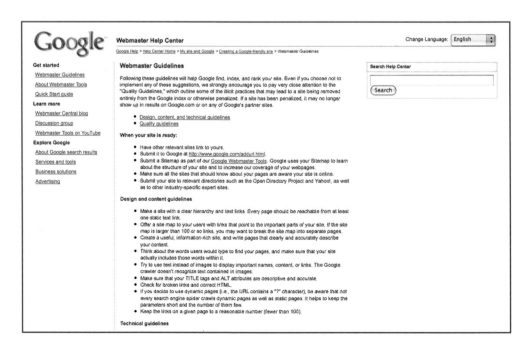

PART

Bigger and better site building

We've already discovered the basics of site building and the importance of planning. Now, we'll bring the two together and see how to build a bigger website.

For this workshop we've decided to build an online portfolio, a kind of digital CV, for the (fictional) writer Angus Fridge. Angus does a bit of everything – TV, radio, newspapers, books – and our site needs to cover everything he does. With our trusty Biro we've sketched out a plan of the site and we think it needs to have the following pages:

- A home page, introducing the site and highlighting anything interesting
- A page telling visitors all about Angus
- A page for Angus's magazine work, with pages for each kind of magazine thing he does
- A page for Angus's newspaper work, again with linked pages on specific kinds of newspaper work
- A page for Angus's radio appearances
- A page for Angus's TV appearances
- A page for Angus's books
- A page for Angus's photography
- A page of frequently asked questions
- A page of contact information

It's a fairly standard structure and it works for all kinds of things – so, for example, a site about your home town could have a welcome page and then pages on eating out, transport, interesting local landmarks, famous local people and so on; a site for a building firm would have pages dedicated to each kind of job, so you might have a page about extensions, one about building new houses, one for interior jobs, one for decking and so on; and a site for a kids' club would have a page with timetables, a page of photos, a page of testimonials and so on.

As you'll see, we don't start putting the pages together immediately. Instead, we'll create an overall look for our website and save it. That way, when we do add new pages they'll use our design automatically – which saves an enormous amount of time.

Once again we'll use Paint.net for our graphics and NetObjects Fusion Essentials for our site building. You can of course use any web editing package to build a site, but we think Fusion Essentials is a good choice for beginners – not least because it's free!

Creating a header image in Paint.net

1

Load Paint.net and click on Image > Canvas Size. Set the width to 800 pixels and the height to 150 pixels. This is a good size for a header image: big enough to look good, but not so big that it dominates the screen.

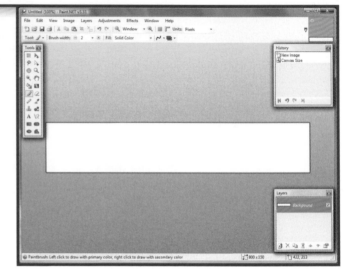

2

We're going to use part of a photograph in our header image. To do this, open the photo in Paint.net and use the selection tool (the dotted box icon in the very top left of the Tools palette) to draw around the whole photo. Click on the Copy icon (or press Ctrl+C) to copy it to the clipboard.

3

Click on Window > Previous Tab to return to your blank header image. Click on Paste. Paint.net will now tell you that your image is much bigger than the canvas size, and give you the choice: expand the canvas to fit the image or keep the canvas size. We want the latter option.

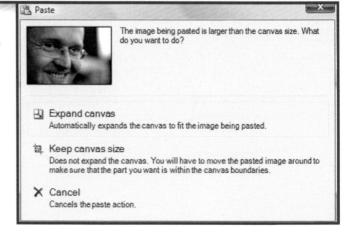

As you can see, only part of our photo is visible – but that's good, because that's the effect we want. Use the mouse to move the image to its desired location and then press Enter to lock it in place.

Now, we want to make the rest of our image black. To do this, click on the Rectangle tool in the Tools palette and then ensure Draw Filled Shape is selected from the Tool toolbar immediately above your image. Press F8 to display the Colors panel (if it isn't already onscreen) and select black.

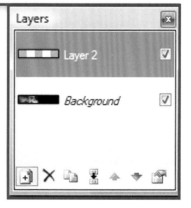

Time for some text. Press F7 to bring up the Layers palette if it isn't already on screen, and click on the New Layer button – it's at the very bottom left of the palette. This adds a new section to your image where you can put things without damaging the bits you've already worked on.

7

Click on the Text tool in the Tools palette, select a colour from
the Colors palette, and click in the black area of your image.
Type some text and then use the toolbar above your image to
change the font and size. You'll see a little box containing arrows
immediately below the text; you can use this to move the text
around.

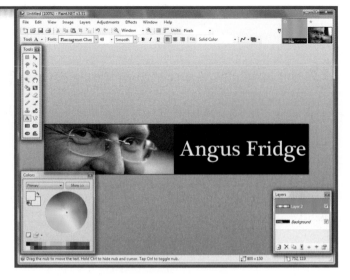

8

Last but not least, let's draw a thin box around our header
image. Click on the Rectangle Tool in the Tools palette and then
select Draw Shape Outline from the toolbar. Draw a box around
the edge of your entire image and then press Enter.

9

Click on File > Save As and give your image a meaningful name
– we're calling ours Angusheader. Save it in the folder containing
the bits and bobs you want to use in your site, changing the file
type to JPEG. Paint.net will now ask you to select the image
quality you need; stick with the default setting of 95%. Close
Paint.net when you're finished.

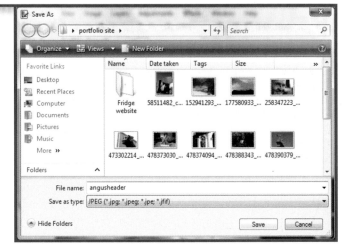

Creating your site design

Let's build our site. Open Fusions Essentials and click on File > New Site > Blank Site. Choose a location for your site files and give the site a meaningful name so you can find it again later. You should now see the Site Structure view, with a single page inside it.

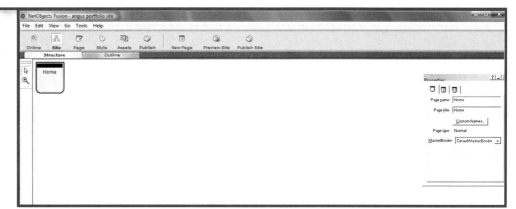

Let's set some ground rules first. Click on Tools > Options > Current Site and you'll see the standard settings for a new web page. We want to make some changes to this. Under New Page Size, change the height to 640 pixels and the width to 800. Under Text Formatting, select the Cascading Style Sheets (CSS) option. This ensures maximum compatibility between your site and all kinds of web browsers. Click on OK when you've done this.

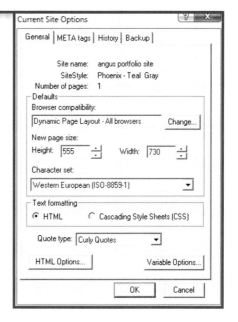

Double-click on the Home page icon to go into page editing mode. As you can see, things aren't quite right: despite choosing a blank site we've got a basic layout and, if you look at the Layout Properties palette at the right of the screen, our page sizes aren't right. Let's change that. Change the width so the number under Layout is 640 and the number under Page is 800, and change the height so the first number is 510 and the second 640.

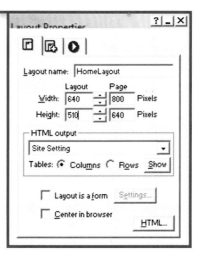

13 That's better. Now, let's get rid of the bits we don't want. Right-click on the Home box at the top of the page and select Delete Object. Do the same with the Built With… image at the bottom. Leave everything else as-is for now.

14 Let's bring in our header image. Click on the image icon (the picture frame in the left-hand toolbar) and draw a box at the top of the screen – but not over the box marked Layout, as Fusion Essentials won't let you. When prompted, select your header image and it will appear on your page.

15 Unfortunately our image has knocked the layout off a bit, but that's easy to fix. Drag the image to the left so that it lines up perfectly with the "Home" box at the left of the screen, then drag the grey boxes in the ruler at the top of the screen to make the Layout box line up with the right of the image.

16 Let's see how that looks. Click on the Page Preview button to see how your page will look in a web browser. Of course, the page is still pretty empty but, as you can see, it's beginning to take shape.

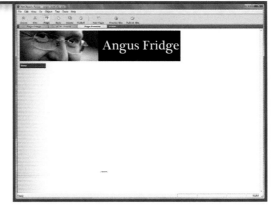

Adding pages and building a photo gallery

Let's add some new pages. Click on the Site button in the toolbar at the top of the screen and then click New Page for each page you'd like to add. Change the name of each new page from "Untitled" to something more interesting.

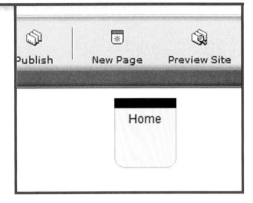

Your new pages should appear in a kind of tree, with Home at the very top. You can add new branches too, so for example we need sub-pages from our Magazines page and our Newspapers page. To add these, select the appropriate page and then click New Page. Once again, rename the pages to something more interesting.

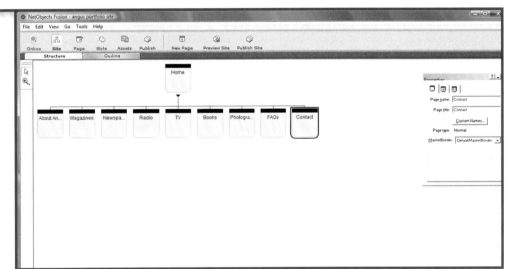

As you can see, Fusion Essentials automatically updates the tree design to take account of your new pages. We're ready to start adding content, so let's do that now. Double-click on a page to edit it. We'll go for the Photography page.

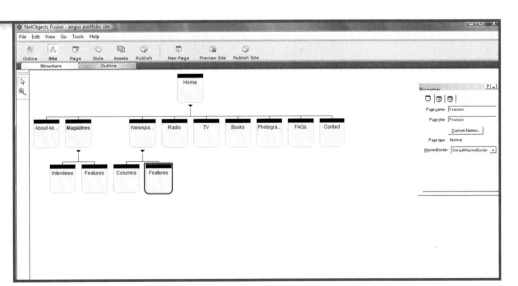

Rather cleverly, Fusion Essentials has automatically updated the navigation bar at the side of the window to include all the pages we've just added – it's a massive time-saver. You'll see that the text links at the bottom of the screen have been updated too.

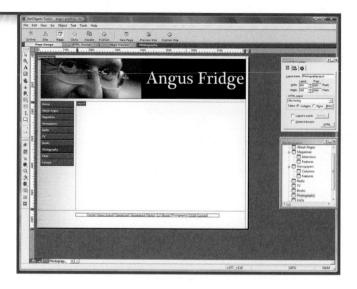

To add content to the page, it's just a matter of choosing the appropriate tool from the toolbar at the left of the screen – so there's an icon for adding text, one for images, and so on. In this case we want to add a Photo Gallery, which is the gold picture icon towards the bottom of the toolbar. Click on it and then draw a box on the page where you want the gallery to go.

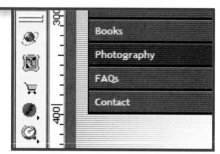

Give your gallery a name and click OK. Browse to the folder containing your photos and select the ones you want to use (hold down Shift to select multiple images or press Ctrl+A to select everything in the folder). Click on Add when you've selected the pictures you want.

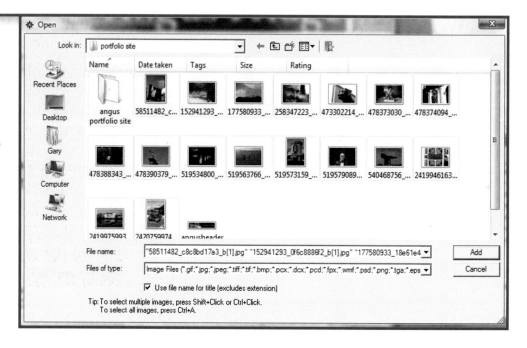

The images will now appear in a list in the left-hand side of the window. Click on each one to give it a meaningful name and description. Once you've done this, click on the Thumbnail Page tab at the top of the window.

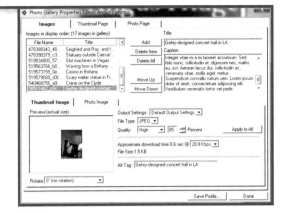

This window enables you to choose how your photos will appear on your page, and it's worth experimenting with the different templates until you find one you like. We'll go with the Drop Shadow template. Now, click on the Photo Page tab to decide how your photographs will look when they're viewed individually.

Once again, we'll go with the Drop Shadow template. If you look towards the top of the window you'll see a number of different layout options; again, it's worth experimenting. We'll go with the fourth option, which displays the title and caption to the right of the image. Use the Format Title and Format Caption buttons to change the text size if you wish, and then click Done to finish.

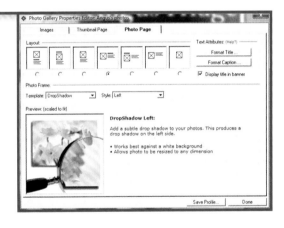

After a few seconds, you should now see the result of your efforts. Nice, isn't it? You can change the appearance of the Photo Gallery at any time by double-clicking on the photos in your page; this will bring up the gallery options for tweaking.

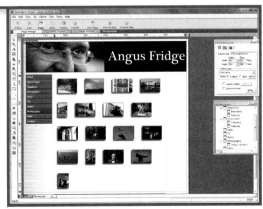

Working with text

27

Let's edit another page. If the Site Navigation palette isn't already visible, press F2 to display it. To edit another page, simply double-click on its name in the Site Navigation palette. This takes you to the appropriate page, ready for editing.

28

For this page, we'll add some text. To do this, click on the Text tool icon in the toolbar at the left of the screen and use it to draw a box inside the Layout area. Once you've done that, it's just a matter of typing your text into the box you've just created.

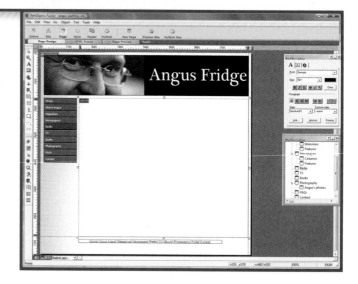

29

By default, your text uses the "normal" style. You can apply other styles for emphasis, and you do that by highlighting the text you want to change and then selecting a Style from the Text Properties box. Try making the first line of your text Heading 1 (H1) format.

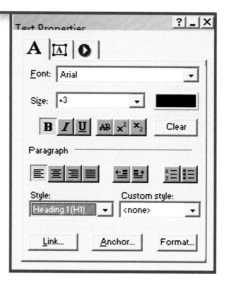

You'll see that the first line of text is now much bigger and bolder than before. It's a step in the right direction, but we can make our text look better – and the changes we make now can be carried across to every page in our website. Click on Text > Edit Text styles to edit the available styles.

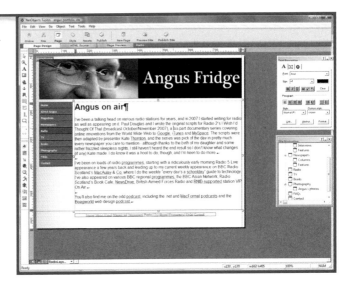

You should now see the Text Styles dialog box as shown here. To edit a style, click on it in the left-hand section of the window and then click on the Edit button. Let's change the H1 style. Click on Heading 1 (H1) in the list of styles and then click Edit.

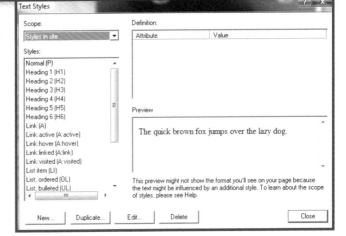

You can change a number of things here. You can change the font, the style – such as bold or italic – and the colour, and you can even make Fusion Essentials change the case of the text – so you can force the text into uppercase irrespective of how it's been typed. Let's make some changes: we'll go for the Georgia font, in bold, with a size of 28 points and we'll make it a dark green colour.

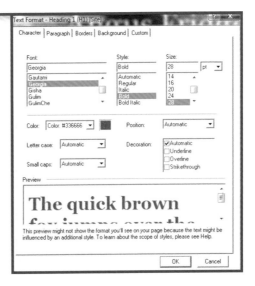

Now, we'll change the Normal (P) style. Once again we'll go for Georgia, but this time we'll choose a font size of 12 points and leave the colour and style set to Automatic. Click on OK when you've done this and then on Close to return to your page.

The changes you've made should now be visible in your page, but the text still looks a little bit cluttered. Let's break up the text a little bit by adding line breaks between some of the sentences. To do this, put the cursor at the beginning of the line you want to move and press the Enter key.

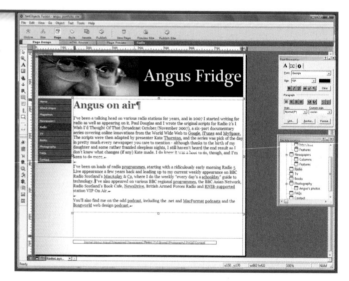

Click on Page Preview to see how the end result looks. It's not bad, but the text is a little bit close to the navigation bar. That's easy to change: just pop back into Page Design view and adjust the text box so its left margin is a little bit further from the navigation bar.

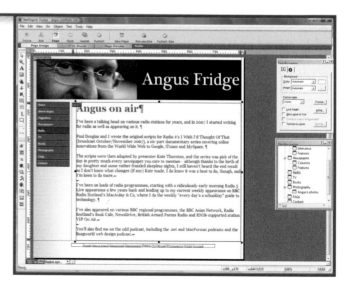

Adding photos and videos from other websites

Wouldn't it be great if you could include YouTube videos or other content in your website? You might be surprised to discover that you can – and it's very easy. In this section, we'll discover how to add videos from YouTube and photos from the photo-sharing site Flickr.

Our intrepid reporter Angus often appears on the BBC's Reporting Scotland *programme, so why not include a clip in his online CV? All we need to do is find the right clip on YouTube and add it to the appropriate page. Here, we've tracked down an old clip of the programme – and it's exactly the one we want.*

If you look to the right of the video you'll see a section headed "Embed". This is the code you need to add this clip to your website. Simply click in the code – the bit starting "<object" – to highlight it and press Ctrl+C to copy it.

Back to Fusion Essentials. Open the TV page, draw a new text box in the layout area and type some introductory text so your visitors know what clip you're going to use. Apply the Heading 1 (H1) style to the first line and leave a couple of blank lines after the end of your text.

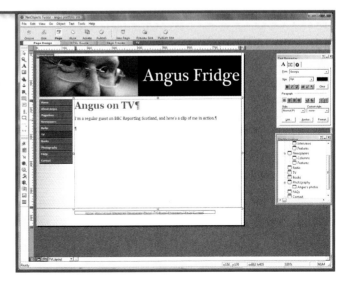

Take a new line and then click on the Add HTML button in the toolbar at the left of the screen. It's second from the bottom and looks like a box with two brackets in it. The Insert HTML box should now appear. Right-click, choose Paste and the YouTube code should now appear in the box.

When you click on OK, it will appear as if nothing has happened: the only sign that you've made a change is a little blue dot at the cursor. That's because Fusion Essentials doesn't display the results of the code when you're in page editing mode; to see it, you'll need to click on Page Preview.

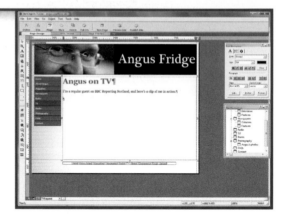

After a few seconds, the YouTube clip should now appear – it won't start playing until you click on it (assuming you're connected to the internet – if you aren't, it won't work at all). You don't have to rely on existing videos, either: if you've got a camcorder you can easily upload your own footage to YouTube and then embed it in your page in exactly the same way.

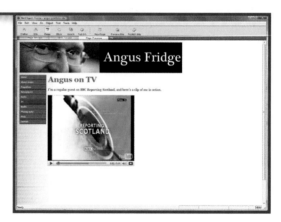

You can also change the way the YouTube player appears in your site. Before you click on the code in YouTube, click the Customize box. This enables you to change the colour of the video player and to specify whether YouTube should suggest similar clips at the end of your chosen footage.

43

You can use the same procedure to add content from other sites. For example, if you store lots of photos on the photo-sharing site Flickr.com, you can easily add a "badge" to encourage people to check out your Flickr photo albums. To do this you'll need to be a member of Flickr and have some photos marked "public". If you do, log in to Flickr and then go to **www.flickr.com/badge.gne**.

44

You have two choices here: a static HTML badge or a smaller, animated Flash badge. The latter is more attractive and that's the one we'd recommend. Select the Flash badge option and then click on the Next button.

45

Flickr will now ask you what photos the badge should display. The default is Yours, which will display photos from all your albums, chosen randomly. If you prefer you can limit the images to a specific album. We'll stick with the default for now, so we'll click on the Next button.

46

Now, you can change the colour scheme. You can see a small preview of the badge at the foot of the screen and this will update to show the effect of any changes. We'll keep the colour scheme as-is but click the No Background and No Border options. Click on Next when you've done this.

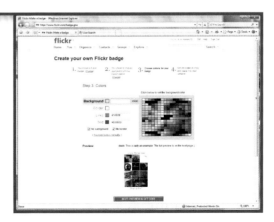

47

Flickr now displays the badge exactly as it will appear on your website and presents you with a box full of code. As with YouTube, it's just a matter of clicking on the code and pressing Ctrl+C to copy it. Return to Fusion Essentials when you've done that.

48

We're going to add the Flickr badge to our Photography page, but we're not going to put it in the main layout section – which means it'll appear on all our pages, not just the Photography one. To do this, we'll draw a text box immediately underneath the navigation buttons and put the badge in that. Once you've drawn the box, click the Insert HTML icon and paste in the Flickr code.

49

As ever, you won't see the results until you click on Page Preview (and as with YouTube, you'll need to be connected to the internet or it won't work). After a few seconds, the badge should appear and start shuffling images around. To move it, just return to page editing mode and move the text box.

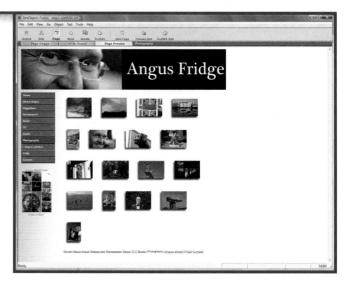

Improving the layout and adding links

So far we've created some fairly simple layouts, but Fusion Essentials is capable of doing much more. In this section, we'll discover how you can improve the way your pages look.

We've added some text to our About Angus page, but now we'll make it look a bit more interesting by adding a picture and sticking it inside our text. Select the image tool (the fourth icon from the top of the toolbar) and draw a box anywhere inside the layout area.

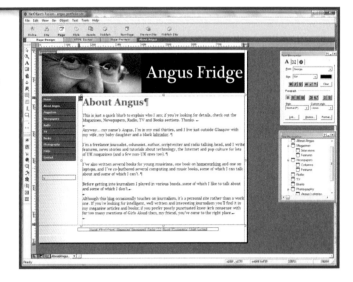

Choose the image you want to use and it will appear inside your text – but as you can see, it looks awful because it's split the text up. We can change this in the Picture Properties palette at the top right of the screen.

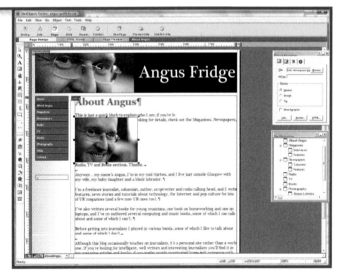

Click on the third tab in the Picture Properties palette and you'll see the Align options. Click on Left Wrap and you'll see your photo move to the left of the layout area, with the text flowing around it. This is exactly what we want and it looks better already.

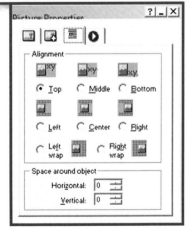

Although our image is in the right place, the text is far too close to it. We can adjust that in the Picture Properties palette: in the Align section, adjust the "Space Around Object" to add some white space around the picture. If you then click on the first tab in the Picture Properties palette and select Stretch, you can resize the image slightly to make it bigger or smaller. Click on Page Preview to see the result.

While Fusion Essentials has automatically created a navigation bar to move between pages, sometimes you might want to add page links in the body text – or link to other sites. Adding links is simple: just highlight the text you'd like to turn into a link and then click the Add Link button in the toolbar on the left.

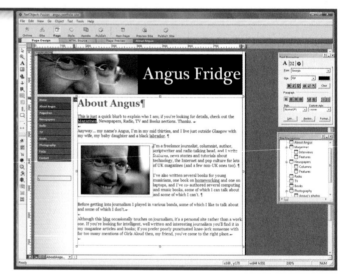

You should now see the Link dialog box. To link to another page in your site, simply select it from the list on the left-hand side of the dialog box and then click on the Link button.

As you can see, the text you highlighted has been turned into a blue hyperlink. When your visitors click the link, they'll be taken to the page you've linked to. Adding external links – that is, links to other websites – is just as easy. Once again you need to highlight the text you want to turn into a link and then click the Add Link button.

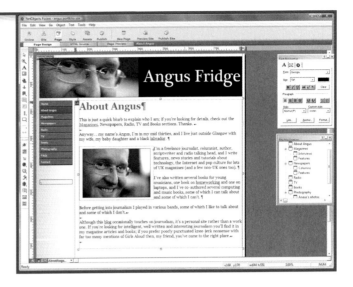

This time, you need to select External Link from the Link Type drop-down at the top of the dialog box. In the New Link boxes, leave the "http://" bit as-is and then type the address in the box to the right – so if you were linking to the Haynes website, you'd enter "www.haynes.co.uk" in here (without the quote marks). Click on Save and then Link to continue.

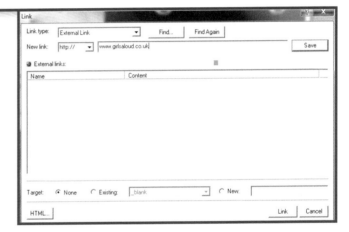

The links won't work in Page Preview mode; to test them, you'll need to use Preview Site to launch your site in a web browser. It's a very good idea to ensure that your links are correct before you publish your site.

Uploading your masterpiece to your web space

Once everything's ready, it's time to publish your site online. To do this, click on the Publish Site button at the top of the screen. The Publish Site dialog appears, and asks where to publish your site. We need to create a new publishing profile, and we do that by clicking on the button with a pencil on it.

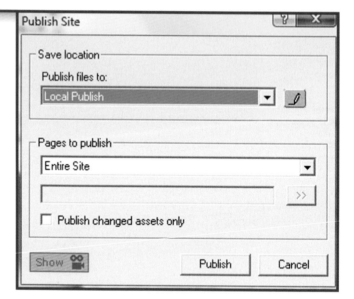

You'll now be asked to choose between remote and local publishing. Remote means on the internet, so choose that option. Now, you'll need to enter the FTP details for your web space. You can get these from your hosting provider. In this example, we use the same Tripod web space we signed up for with our first website.

Fusion Essentials saves FTP information on a per-site basis, which means if you enter the information here you'll need to enter it again if you build another site. To fix this, click on Save as Global Profile, give the profile a name and then click on Save.

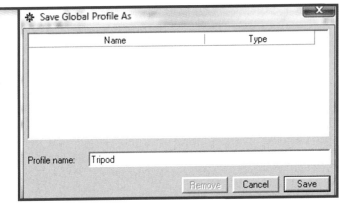

You'll now return to the Publish Settings dialog. Click on OK and you'll see the Publish Site screen. If you're updating a busy site, tick the "Published changed assets only" – this compares the files on your computer with the ones on your web space and only uploads the files that are different. It's a huge time saver. Click on Publish to continue.

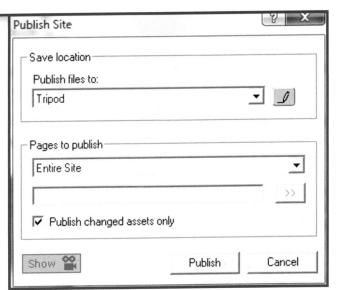

After a while – ranging from seconds to minutes, depending on how big your site is – you'll see the File Transfer Is Complete message. You can now visit your website from any machine; in this example our web address is a Tripod one – **members.lycos.co.uk/ourusername** *– but if you've bought a domain name and commercial web space it'll be at* **www.yourdomain.co.uk** *(where "yourdomain.co.uk" is the actual domain name you've gone for, such as "bertiebloggs.co.uk").*

PART **3** BUILD YOUR OWN WEBSITE
Blogging on

To blog or not to blog

So far we've looked at building a normal web page, but there's another way to put your words on the web: blogs. Blogs – short for "web logs" – are a phenomenon, with blog search engine Technorati tracking some 112.8 million of them. So what are they and why should you care?

A blog is a kind of website, but it has a slightly different approach to traditional sites. Instead of a home page and individual subject pages, a blog is more like a diary – so the most recent thing you've published, known as a blog post, appears at the top of your front page. Blogs can be about anything: there are gadget blogs and game blogs, business blogs, political blogs, health blogs, fashion blogs... if you can imagine it, somebody's probably running a blog about it.

A good example of the difference between a normal website and a blog is found at the *Guardian* newspaper, which has a traditional website as well as lots of blogs. If you go to **www.guardian.co.uk**, you'll see a fairly normal news website, with a home page and lots of sections. However, if you go to the Comment Is Free section (**www.guardian.co.uk/commentisfree**), you'll see something a bit different. There are still articles, but they're not the end of the story: on Comment Is Free, it's the reader comments that matter. And that's the main difference between a website and a blog: a website is something you look at but a blog is something you interact with. The whole point of a blog post is to encourage comments from your visitors.

The *Guardian* newspaper has a pretty typical website – there's a home page and lots of specific sections. It's not hugely different from the websites you'd see in the 1990s.

The *Guardian*'s Comment Is Free site is rather different. It still has articles, but they're there to start conversations with readers. Blogs are all about the comments.

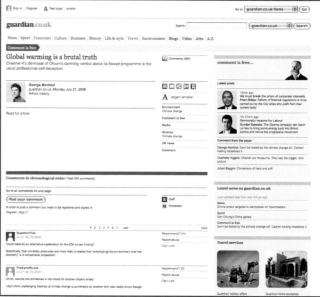

Here are the key differences between blogs and normal websites.

- **You don't need web space:** If you've got web space, you can install a blogging system on it – but if you haven't, you don't need it. For example, if you use Blogger.com or WordPress.com for your blog, your pages are stored on Blogger.com or WordPress.com.

- **You don't need software:** Almost every blogging system works in your web browser, which means you can update your blog from any PC without having to download software.

- **You don't need any design skills:** When you create a blog, you can choose from a selection of professionally designed templates – and you can then tweak the design to get rid of any bits you don't want.

- **You don't need money:** Signing up with a big-name blogging system won't cost you a penny. Blogger.com, WordPress.com and rival blogging services give you everything you need for free.

- **You don't need time:** Blogging is more like writing a letter than building a website: you simply type your words into the editing box, hit Publish and the results are online instantly.

- **You don't need to know what you're doing:** Blogging systems are designed to be user friendly, so they take care of the technical stuff for you.

- **You get to meet new and interesting people:** Blogs include commenting systems that enable your readers to leave comments. Blog posts often become giant conversations: a recent post on our own blog ended up with 74 comments from all kinds of people.

- **You don't need a computer:** If your mobile phone has a web browser, you can blog from your mobile – and even if it doesn't, many blogging platforms enable you to write posts on your mobile and email them to your blog. As soon as you click Publish, your blog post is available to anybody on the internet.

With many blogging systems, you can update your blog from your mobile phone. It's just a matter of writing a post and clicking Publish. The results will be online in seconds.

The famous five

There's no such thing as a standard blog, as you'll discover when you look at five of the better-known blogs: Robot Wisdom, Scaryduck, Boing Boing, MetaFilter and Waxy.

Robot Wisdom (www.robotwisdom.com)

Robot Wisdom is one of the internet's most famous blogs and it follows a simple formula: every day Jorn Barger posts a big list of links with a very short explanation of what each one is. For example, a typical link might say "Wal-Mart drops local paper after too-honest report". If you want to know the full story, you'll need to click on the link. Robot Wisdom is blogging at its most minimalist.

Robot Wisdom is blogging at its most basic: a collection of links with a very short description of each one.

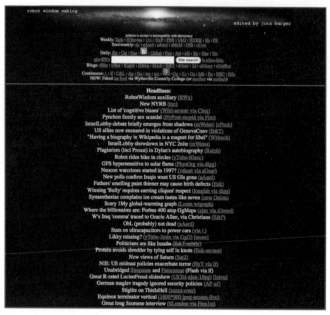

Scaryduck (http://scaryduck.blogspot.com)

Scaryduck is a good example of the blog as an online diary, and describes itself as "being in the main an account of the interesting and varied life of Scaryduck: genius, gentleman explorer, French cabaret chantoose [sic] and small bets placed". It's a very British blog, with regular updates on the author's adventures interspersed with the odd rant and lots of humour.

Scaryduck is a very British blog, with self-deprecating humour and the odd rant about life's little irritations.

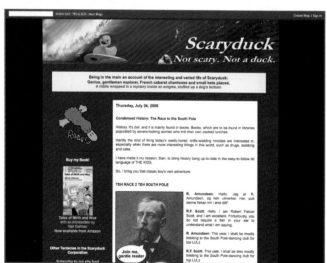

Boing Boing (www.boingboing.net)

Run by a handful of tech journalists, Boing Boing bills itself as "a directory of wonderful things" and provides links to the more interesting, worrying or plain weird stories on other sites.

Boing Boing is good at finding the wackier side of technology, although some of its content is a little geeky for our tastes.

Waxy.org (www.waxy.org)

Andy Baio's blog covers technology and pop culture in a clever way. While the main blog consists of longish articles, there's also a sidebar at the right of the screen that provides links with a few words of commentary, Robot Wisdom-style. It's a good way of blogging about lots of different things without intimidating readers or giving them sore eyes.

Waxy.org manages to combine long articles with lots of links in a way that won't give you a splitting headache.

MetaFilter (www.metafilter.com)

Most blogs are written by one person, or by a small group of people. MetaFilter, on the other hand, is put together by tens of thousands of members. It covers every conceivable subject and it's one of our favourite weblogs.

MetaFilter works because of its clever structure. Stories on the front page are single paragraph affairs, and each one links to a dedicated page where MeFites (the users of MetaFilter) discuss the story. The blog is broken into sections, so there's AskMe for general questions ("How do I get red wine out of carpet stains?" "What's the best way to quit smoking?"), MetaTalk for discussions about the nuts and bolts of MetaFilter itself, and the main MetaFilter site for newsworthy and interesting things. Members are expected to follow some simple rules: don't post things we've all seen before, don't indulge in blatant self-promotion, and don't simply regurgitate things you've seen elsewhere on the internet. Because most people do follow these rules, MetaFilter's always worth reading.

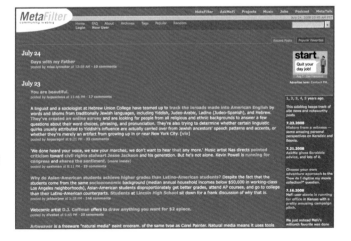

With tens of thousands of members, MetaFilter is one of the biggest and best community weblogs on the internet.

Blog builders

The popularity of blogs means that there's no shortage of companies trying to persuade you to use their system for your blog. The available options tend to fall into two camps: simple, beginner-friendly packages that do all the hard work for you and all-singing, all-dancing blog platforms that can do everything but feed your dog. In the first camp, you'll find Blogger.com, WordPress.com, Windows Live Spaces and dozens of other instant-publishing efforts; in the latter camp, there's WordPress.org, Movable Type and various paid-for packages.

The famous five we've just looked at use a variety of tools: Scaryduck uses Blogger.com and Waxy.org uses Movable Type.

So which is right for you? If all you need is the basics, Blogger.com ticks all the boxes: it's free, it's easy to use and it covers all the essentials of blogging. However, we prefer the rival WordPress.com. It's slightly – but not dramatically – more complicated than Blogger, but the results are more impressive and it's surprisingly powerful for a free package.

For more advanced blogging, we're big fans of WordPress.org – not least because you can easily import old blog posts from Blogger.com or WordPress.com – but Movable Type has an army of loyal users too. Ultimately, though, it comes down to personal preference: most blogging systems work in the same way, so the best system is the one that feels most comfortable to you. In the following tutorials, we'll be using WordPress.com, but you'll find that things are very similar in Blogger and other systems.

There's another option. If you only want to post snippets of interesting things, a site such as Tumblr (**www.tumblr.com**) might be right up your street. It's designed for quick and easy sharing of interesting things such as photos, quotes or passing thoughts; while it's not really up to the job of long, text-heavy posts, it's perfect as a kind of digital scrapbook.

Movable Type is probably overkill for basic blogging, but it's an enormously powerful system for building and managing big blogs.

The free Blogger.com is easy to use and produces decent results, but it's not the only free blogging platform available.

PART 6

Making your blog count

Whether you're creating a brand new blog or looking for ways of improving one you've already started, you can learn a lot from the other blogs on the web. From the good ones you'll learn the importance of being original, writing regularly, expressing yourself clearly and finding interesting topics to post about. From the bad, you'll learn to avoid sloppy writing, inconsistency of tone and failing to respect other bloggers and potential readers.

You should also heed the advice of successful bloggers, many of whom reveal their own tips and tricks through their blogs. If there's one thing bloggers like writing about more than their chosen theme, it's their blogs. But don't take anything you discover by reading other people's blogs, or anything you read in the rest of this chapter, as fixed and unbending. In the end there are no rules. The really successful blog is not the one with the punchiest writing, fanciest presentation and hottest news; it's the one that readers keep coming back to. If you can click with your readers, they'll keep you on the right track through their feedback and personal contributions.

What should your blog be about?

For some, the subject of their blog chooses itself. It's an issue they care deeply about and they want to share their opinions and ideas with a wider public. You'll find blogs concentrating on

Who would have thought the notion of recording the 14 miles of above-ground scenery on the route of London's Circle Line would result in an award-winning blog, especially as the photos are taken with a primitive pinhole camera: **www.nyclondon/blog**.

Neil Gaiman, hard-working novelist and comic book author, is a shameless self-publicist who writes almost exclusively about himself yet has one of the most frequented blogs on the web. Don't try this yourself unless you're already famous: **www.neilgaiman.com**.

serious issues such as terrorism, poverty and human rights, but there are just as many covering personal, but still deeply felt, obsessions such as soaps and celebrities, rock climbing and rock music.

At the other end of the scale there are blogs designed solely to give the author a form of self-expression, and where there is no cohesive theme other than the author's desire to communicate about anything and everything. Blogs like these can be riveting if you have the time and talent to nurture them; but unless you're already famous for doing something else, it's unlikely you'll draw many readers to a personal site even if it's brilliantly written.

Between the two extremes, people write blogs for all sorts of reasons. Some do it to keep in touch with family and friends around the world, and others as a way of supplementing their income by including pay-per-click advertisements. Commercial organisations use blogs to promote their products, charities use them to promote their causes and writers use them to sell their books. Blogs are also written to make friends, to while away the time, to keep minds active, to learn about computers and to practise writing skills.

Personal and public blogs

Whatever it is that's inspiring you to create a blog will almost certainly help you pick a suitable subject to write about. If the blog is primarily intended for friends and family then the subject matter will be you, your loved ones, your jobs, home, pets, holidays and pastimes, and it doesn't really matter how well you write because your audience just wants to keep in touch. However, don't expect anybody who stumbles across your blog to come back in a hurry, even if your children are budding geniuses, your dog can walk on its hind legs and you've just been promoted at work.

If your blog is a mercenary attempt to generate income through pay-per-click advertising, the theme must be related to the advertising you intend to carry. The same holds true for commercial sites too. It's no good creating a fascinating blog about the rock music scene if your product is hand-made cheeses. Then again, neither would you want to limit yourself to cheese-making as a topic. Cheese-making doesn't change much from day to day and wouldn't benefit from the journal-style blog approach, so a blog focussing on healthy eating, gourmet recipes

How do you turn a company blog promoting a sheet metal-working concern in the wilds of Lancashire into an award-winning blog? Find out at **www.butlersheetmetal.com/tinbasherblog**.

or modern lifestyles would be more suitable. It would also be easier to maintain because there's no shortage of constantly updated links on these topics.

Even better from a marketing point of view would be a blog called Hard Cheese, which could regale its readers with strange tales of coincidence and ill-luck, and be written with tongue firmly in cheek. It has the potential to attract a wider range of readers than a food-related site, and is the sort of subject likely to generate its own material thanks to readers' contributions.

A long-term endeavour

Whatever subject you decide to hang your blog around, make sure it's something that will maintain your interest and that of its potential visitors. Ideally you'll be updating it every day, so it's important to remain enthusiastic about the topic, especially as it takes a long time to build an interesting archive of past articles and posts that will serve as a bedrock for the daily journal entries. While you may yearn to own a blog that hits the news and becomes an overnight success, such sites are rare and they're nearly always tied to major news stories such as wars, scandals and crimes. Keeping a topical site going when interest in the subject starts to wane could turn into a very hard slog.

Boing Boing (**http://boingboing.net**) is a collaborative blog calling itself a directory of wonderful things, e.g. lingerie for cows and rugs patterned like giant slices of salami. Sites like these thrive because of the active participation of their readers.

Keeping your blog up to date

PART 3

Once you know what you're going to write about you need to keep in touch with what's in the news and what people are talking about in your chosen field. Regardless of how cleverly your blog page is put together and how many fancy features and tricks it incorporates, what keeps readers coming back are the links you find to other sites and the comments you make about how you see the world.

Really Simple Syndication

Obviously, it's impossible to keep up to date by idly browsing the web because it's such a big place that you might easily miss stories of great interest. With almost every kind of print and broadcast media also directing much of its output to the web you need some way of cutting through the mountains of media fluff to locate items genuinely relevant to your blog. The primary technique is the use of RSS feeds. RSS stands for Really Simple Syndication and is a way of having updates from websites you're interested in delivered to your computer without you having to visit the site and trawl through stuff you've seen before. Not every site offers RSS feeds but those that do include all the major news gathering organisations including CNN and the BBC, plus

Bloglines (**www.bloglines.com**) is an online treasure chest for bloggers. You can build a blog, search other blogs and handle RSS feeds all from the same site.

The great thing about Google Alerts (**www.googlealert.com**) is that you don't have to join anything. Simply provide a valid email address to which search results can be sent.

New postings in selected Yahoo groups can be directed to your email address, but choose your groups carefully or you might be overwhelmed by trivia.

Some bloggers add buttons to their blogs making it easier for you to subscribe to blog updates via RSS. Incredibly, this selection all came from the same site.

leading world newspapers and magazines. In addition, there are RSS feeds from other blogs and from websites like How Stuff Works.

Subscriptions to RSS feeds are free, as is most of the software you need to read them. Technically such programs are called aggregators but they are commonly referred to as feeders or readers. You can choose between an RSS reader that displays your chosen feeds on a dedicated web page that you visit or one that runs on your PC as a stand-alone program. If you use a web browser such as Firefox or Opera, you can even read RSS feeds in your browser without having to go to a special web page.

News delivered to your inbox

Another way of keeping up to date is to register your email address with websites that send news, information and updates directly to your inbox. Not all websites offer this kind of service but many of them do. For sites that don't, you can use Google Alerts instead. A Google Alert is a pre-defined Google search, the results of which are emailed to you on a regular basis. You can choose to receive Google Alerts weekly, daily or as they happen. When you receive an Alert it contains clickable links you can follow, just like the results of an interactive Google search.

Two other services that that will keep your inbox supplied with regularly updated and relevant material are the special interest groups operated by Yahoo and Google. These groups, which offer a web-based alternative to the unregulated world of Usenet news groups, can be browsed online or you can have group updates sent to you by email, either as daily digests or when new posts are made. There are millions of Yahoo groups to choose from, and even though many of them are almost inactive there's a healthy number that are both on-topic and thriving. Google has hundreds of thousands of groups and if you don't find what you're looking for you can create a Google Group of your own.

Three ways of handling RSS feeds

In the following step-by-step guides, you'll learn different ways of subscribing to RSS feeds so you can keep up to date with what's happening on selected websites and in other people's blogs. The first workshop describes the use of a dedicated RSS reader working independently of a web browser. The second demonstrates how to use an online service (in this case Newsgator) to locate and read RSS feeds. The third shows how Opera (**www.opera.com**), one of the alternative browsers to Internet Explorer, can view RSS feeds by treating them just like any other message.

Setting up and using FeedReader

*There are plenty of dedicated RSS readers to choose from. This workshop uses one called FeedReader. Being open source software, it's completely free and, at only 1.5MB, it takes less than five minutes to download even on a slower dial-up connection. Go to **www.feedreader.com** to get the latest version.*

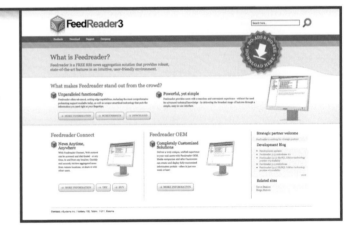

Double click on the downloaded file to install it. After installation FeedReader launches itself automatically. Around 20 feeds are pre-installed so you can start using it straight away. In the left-hand pane, double click on the News category to view all the headlines available from all the News feeds, and then click on BBC News to limit the display of headlines to only those from the BBC.

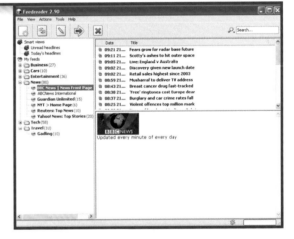

Click any of the headlines in the top right-hand pane and you'll see a summary of the selected article in the lower right-hand pane. To view the entire article click Read On. While you're doing this, don't be surprised to see pop-up messages in the lower right-hand corner of the screen announcing additional headlines as the BBC makes them available. To expand a news story to fill the FeedReader window use the F11 key, which invokes so-called Aquarium view. To return to normal view, simply press F11 again.

4

To add a new RSS feed to FeedReader, go to the web page of the site you want to add and look for an XML or RSS button (you'll find one at the bottom of the page at **www.telegraph.co.uk***). When you click the button it takes you to a page listing all the feeds available. Tick the box to show you accept the terms and conditions, and then click the UK News button.*

5

This is the code that FeedReader or any other RSS reader can use to display UK news headlines from the Daily Telegraph, *but the only part you need to concern yourself with is the URL at the top. Select this and press Ctrl+C to copy it to the Windows clipboard.*

6

Switch to FeedReader and open the File menu, then click Add Feed. In the Add new feed dialogue box press Ctrl+V to paste the link you copied in step 5. Click Next. Select News as the folder where the feed should be created, and then click Finish. Feeds can be reorganised by dragging them into new folders, or deleted by right-clicking to select Delete current feed from the context menu.

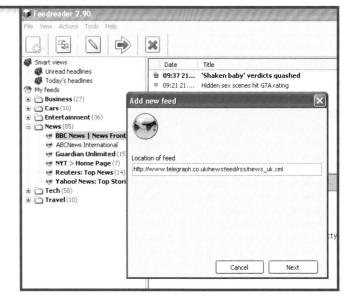

1

Go to **www.newsgator.com** *and click on the "New User?" button. Pick a user name and password, then provide a contact name and email address. Click Next. Tick the box next to any subject area you're interested in and make sure you also tick the "I agree to the NewsGator Online Terms of Service" box. Click on Next to continue.*

2

After a few seconds, the NewsGator Online Reader will launch in your web browser. The feeds (if any) you chose when you signed up will be displayed at the left of the screen. The numbers in brackets tell you how many unread stories are in each feed or group of feeds. Click on the plus sign next to NewsGator Starter Pack to see the feeds in that group.

3

When you click on a feed in the left-hand side of the window, NewsGator displays its contents in the main screen. To see the original web page an article came from, simply click on its headline (right click if you want to open it in a new browser tab).

You can add new feeds in several ways. If you've copied the URL of an RSS feed from a website (see steps 4 and 5 in the previous workshop), you can add it to Newsgator by clicking Add Feeds and then selecting the URL & Import tab. Paste the URL into the Feed panel and click the Add Feed button. Click the Newsgator Online tab to return to what you were doing.

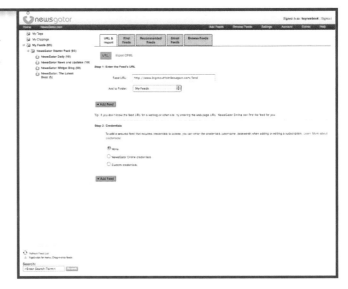

When you don't already have a URL the easiest way of adding new feeds is to use Newsgator's built-in search engine. Click Add Feeds and then select the Find Feeds tab. You may then browse through a categorised list of topics or find feeds by entering a search term. After searching you can click on the name of a site to view the site itself, or click on Subscribe to add the site's feed to your list.

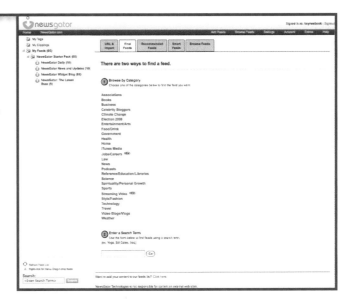

To remove feeds you no longer require, click on Settings and then on My Feeds. To delete a feed, simply click on the red cross to the right of that feed's name. If you wish, you can also use this screen to group feeds into folders: click on Organize Folders, select the feeds you want to organise and then click on Move. After you click the Move button, you'll be prompted to name the new folder.

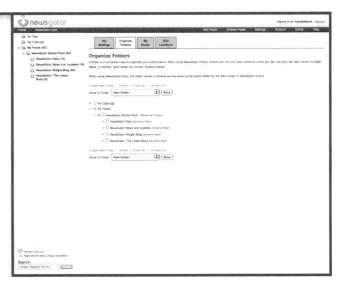

Using the Opera browser as a news feed reader

Here's how to add a news feed to Opera using an RSS or XML button displayed on a web page. Go to **www.pitpass.com** *and look at the top-right corner of the page. Click on the RSS button. When a pop up message asks you if you wish to subscribe, click Yes. The display will almost immediately change to Opera's email-style view showing PitPass headlines in the top pane. Click on any of these to view a link to the full story in the lower pane.*

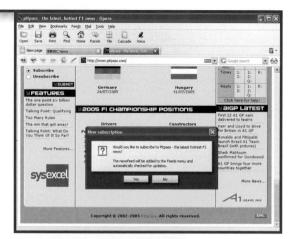

To add a news feed to Opera when you already know the URL of the feed, open Opera's Feeds menu and select Manage Feeds. Click New and type (or paste) the URL into the Address panel. If you want to personalise the name of the feed, remove the tick against "Get name from feed" and type a new one into the Name panel. Use the drop-down list to choose how frequently you want to receive updates, then click OK.

You can delete feeds and set other options by clicking Manage Feeds on the Feeds menu. By removing the tick from a feed you suppress its display on the Feeds menu without actually deleting it. To permanently remove a feed, click to select the feed and then press the Delete button.

To change the name of a feed or the frequency with which you receive updates from it, select the feed and click Edit. This displays the properties of the link (as in step 2), which can be modified. If you use Opera as your email client, it's also possible to forward headlines and links to others who may be interested. Simply right-click on an item in the top pane, select Forward, then type the recipient's address and click Send.

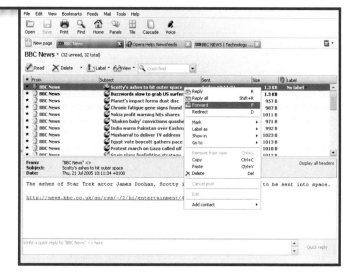

The importance of good writing

Successful blogs tend to have two key attributes: they're interesting, and they're easy to read. Badly written blog posts can be an ordeal to wade through, and unless your visitors are really patient they're unlikely to hang around your blog for very long. We're not suggesting you sit with a dictionary or a style guide when you post – informal, punchy writing is one of the things that makes blogs so much fun – but the better your writing, the better your blog will be.

Some bloggers craft their posts in word-processing software, using the spelling and grammar checkers to ensure that every paragraph is perfect. That's probably overkill – especially since most web browsers now have basic spell-checkers that let you know when you've made a howler – but there are some rules that are worth bearing in mind whenever you blog. You can take our tips to heart or you can ignore them completely: after all, if what you have to say is fascinating and relevant it will find an audience no matter how you choose to express it.

Then again, the following tips can make a good blog even better.

- Imagine you're writing a letter to a close friend rather than composing the leader column for *The Times*. Informal, friendly writing is always more fun to read than stiff, formal prose.
- Keep it short. Long sentences and huge blocks of text are hard to read on a computer screen and even worse on a mobile phone or pocket PC.
- Try to develop your own style rather than copying somebody else's. Your readers will get to know your style and will come back for more of it – and they won't expect it to chop and change.
- Don't use jargon, obscure terms or acronyms unless you're absolutely certain that all your readers will know what you're on about.

Mark Bernstein thinks most readers will forgive punctuation and spelling mistakes. Check out the rest of his advice on writing for the web at **www.alistapart.com/articles/writeliving**.

This sort of post might amuse close friends but is unlikely to bring the casual reader back for more. To spare her blushes, there's no URL for this one.

WEDNESDAY, JULY 13, 2005

wednesday woes.

sigh. just recieved the cc bills and the amount is slightly more than expected. it just went up to an amount i could jolly well get a speedy 25 (not that i like to have 1). seriously, i didn't buy much over at taiwan. i merely went crazy over the blings and shoes (i bought a good n cheap 10 pairs back!). that's all. hongkees have better taste. sigh, there goes my ikea white side table and the matching vanity table plus the lv le cherry pochette. i dare not go on because it will reflect how many lemmings i actually have. bad, very bad.

anyhoos, 3 more days people. at least, i get to enjoy good food, fab company and kickass musik!

Stuart Hughes, BBC journalist and prize-winning blogger, demonstrates the power of short sentences. Check out his style at **http://stuarthughes.blogspot.com**.

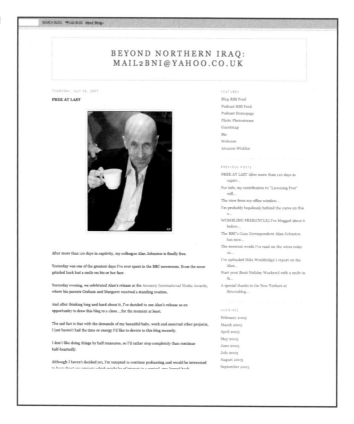

- Don't be afraid to use everyday language, but avoid local slang. Your blog readers are likely to come from all over the world, so avoid using terms that won't mean anything to people who don't live in the same town as you.
- If you feel strongly about something, don't hold back – but don't let it turn into a big rant either. One or two punchy paragraphs will get the message across much more effectively than a big long ramble.
- Avoid txt-speak, internet acronyms ("LOL" and so on), clichés and exclamation marks wherever possible, unless you're using them for comedic effect.
- Avoid hyperbole (again, unless you're doing it to be funny).
- Get to the point. Readers have short attention spans, so they won't appreciate a long introduction or a post that meanders on and on without really coming to a conclusion.
- Don't assume your readers are regulars. Many of your readers will be first-time visitors who found one of your blog posts via a web search, so they will have no idea who you are or what you've written in the past.
- Avoid the passive voice. "We decided…" is much punchier than "It was decided that we…".
- Don't waffle. Remove unnecessary words and details that don't matter. Why use 200 words to say something that can be said in one sentence?

Most importantly of all:

- Keep writing. The more you write, the easier it gets and the better your writing becomes.

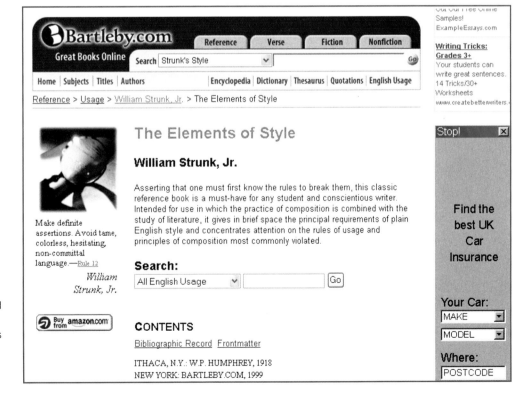

Almost any blog can be improved if its writer checks out the free online version of William Strunk's Elements of Style (**www.bartleby.com/141**), which is full of practical examples.

BLOGGING ON

24 tips for a successful blog

A blog becomes successful by being:

- Mentioned and linked to in other blogs
- Chosen as a site of the day by a blog host
- Found by popular search engines
- Recommended by word of mouth
- Given an award of some kind
- Picked up by the mainstream media

The chances of these things happening depend on how closely you follow the unwritten rules of blogging. Nobody will link to your blog unless you've got something interesting to say and you say it well, but your blog must also show regard for blog etiquette, which is really just another way of saying you've got to respect both your readers and your fellow bloggers.

We've organised 20 tips into a list of dos and don'ts with a bonus at the end in the form of suggestions for what to do on days when you can't think of anything to blog about. The tips are in no particular order, and they're all aimed at turning your blog into one that people will enjoy reading and one that stays on the right side of the law. There's nothing in here about making money, marketing or getting your blog listed by the big search engines, but if this is what you're after you'll find plenty of stuff on the web. Start with a search on "Boosting Google rankings" and take it from there.

If you can't think of a catchy title for your blog, take a look through the top 100 blogs listed at **www.technorati.com**. Two titles in the current list are "Best Page in the Universe" and "Something Awful'.

Do:

- Give your blog a catchy and unique title, and preferably one that's at least obliquely relevant to the theme of your blog. People who like your blog will bookmark it, but they've got to find it first.

- Write to please an audience of one: yourself. Constantly ask yourself whether you'd still be reading your blog if somebody else had written it. If the answer is yes, you're a success.

- Compose your blog in easily-digestible chunks. Blog readers are browsers, and if they want to read long screeds of text they'll pick up a book. Keep sentences short, include bullet points and use descriptive headings to split up long sections.

- Post regularly. Every day is the target (some people post even more frequently) but if this isn't possible, aim for at least twice a week. One of British prime minister Harold Wilson's most enduring remarks is that a week is a long time in politics. In the blogosphere, it's even longer, and a blog with no activity for a week starts to drop off most people's radar screens.

- Include an email address in your blog but not your usual private one. Set up a separate address just for your blog. It's bound to attract a certain amount of spam even if you use spam-dodging tricks such as writing **mary@REMOVETHISuk.pippex.net**, but a separate email address can be changed as often as you like without affecting your regular email.

- Answer all polite emails sent by individuals in good faith. You can ignore the rest.

- Warn people if you provide a link to any web page or blog that contains material they may find offensive or disturbing. As a rule of thumb, this means anything you'd be shocked to see on the front page of a reputable newspaper.

- Credit other bloggers whenever you can. If you use a link you found in somebody else's blog, say where you got it, and whenever you mention a blogger by name it's good manners to include a link to their blog.

- Include relevant pictures in your blog. They add colour and break up the page. But don't go over the top because not everybody has a broadband connection. Always crop and resample pictures to achieve the smallest possible file size, providing a link to a higher resolution version of the picture where necessary.

- Tell people before you go on holiday or if for any other reason you will not be updating your blog for a while. If you expect readers to come back, announce the date on which you'll be resuming regular posts and stick to it come hell or high water.

Don't:

- Pass off speculation or opinion as fact. People are interested in your comments but you've got to make it clear when you're commenting and when you're reporting.

- Use misleading headlines in your posts. Headlines are likely to get picked up by search engines and readers get justifiably angry if they visit your blog after searching for information and find you writing about what you had for breakfast.

- Post when you are angry. If you're feeling passionate about something, write a blog entry by all means, but don't post it until you've calmed down and read it again.

- Attack other bloggers personally. By all means attack what they say, but only by providing reasoned arguments, not insults.

- Rewrite what other bloggers have said. Make a comment and attribution instead, always linking to the original article.

- Rewrite, edit or delete your old posts or archives. If you regret something you've previously posted, add a comment to this effect or make an apology. An inconsistent blog has no credibility and neither does its author.

- Lose potential readers by getting over-involved in cross-blog chatter. This may interest you but it's a turn-off for new visitors.

- Give out personal information about anybody (including email addresses and telephone numbers) – unless of course they've published this information themselves.

- Steal bandwidth from other bloggers by linking to pictures and multimedia material stored on their sites. Transfer files to your own server and link to them there.

- Use pictures to which you do not own the rights, especially if your blog has a commercial element. Remember that royalty-free does not mean payment-free, and don't assume you can use a picture just because it is included on a clip-art CD. Copying pictures from books and magazines is another no–no: just because you scan a picture doesn't make it yours. On the positive side you'll find plenty of pictures in the public domain or usable through a Creative Commons agreement at **www.flickr.com** and

Flickr is not only a source of millions of free-to-use images, it incorporates a one-click "Blog This" option that adds pictures to your blog (**www.flickr.com**).

At **http://creativecommons.org** you can search for pictures, audio, video and literary works that you may freely add to your blog.

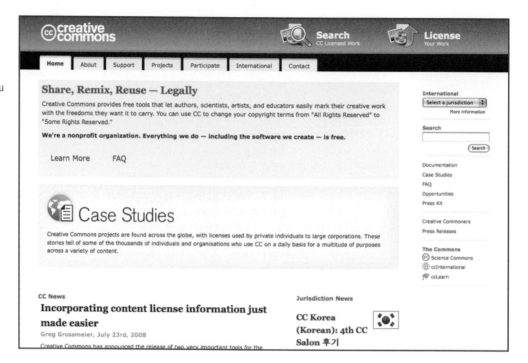

http://creativecommons.org. Whenever you publish a picture in your blog, regardless of its copyright status, remember to include an attribution saying where you got it and from whom.

● Write something that could get you into trouble. Some bloggers have lost their jobs after writing unflattering things about their employers; writers of explicit blogs have been publicly unmasked, leading to red faces and in some cases, job losses; and still others have been sued for writing untrue things about famous people. Under UK law, which applies on the internet as well as in the real world, you can be prosecuted for repeating a libel. If someone else says something horrible about someone and you repeat their claim – or one of your blog commenters does and you don't delete it – you can be sued too.

● Assume that nobody you know reads your blog. Friends, family and admirers could well be regular readers, so don't post anything you wouldn't want them to know about.

● Write something you might regret later. Even if you delete a blog post, it could still hang around the internet for eternity – for example, the Wayback Machine at **www.archive.org** keeps copies of long-deleted web pages, Google keeps copies of indexed files and people can and do save web pages so they can refer to them later. It's always worth asking "could I possibly regret posting this?" before you hit the Publish button. If in doubt, leave it out.

● Blog about or upload photos or videos of friends or family without their permission. Not everybody appreciates publicity, and that funny story or video might be extremely embarrassing for them.

What if there's nothing to write about?

Just as conventional print and broadcast media organisations have their silly seasons, there'll be times when nothing seems to be happening in connection with your blog, leaving you wondering what to write about. One approach is simply to skip making new entries until something catches your eye. After all, there's no law that says you have to blog every day. On the other hand, there are lots of things you can do to tide you over until things pick up.

One solution is to write about personal matters instead of sticking strictly to the theme of your blog. Your readers will probably be keen for an insight into your life when you're not blogging. Another possibility is to post a picture and talk about that, or skim through your online archives and find an existing post you can usefully update.

One of the things newspapers do on slow news days is to instigate a poll and publish the results. This usually involves interviewing a handful of passers-by on the street outside the office. You can do something similar by putting questions in your blog and asking your readers to contribute by email or through online comments, and publishing the results will give you something to write about on another day. In a similar vein you could write a post inviting your readers to comment on the blog itself, asking them whether you should change the screen template, find a new host, use more (or fewer) pictures, or whether they know any good sites you should add to your blogroll.

Perhaps one of the reasons you can't find anything new to write about is because you're always looking for news in the same places. Try widening your searches for on-topic news, or go to one of the popular websites like **www.snopes.com** (urban legends), **www.breakthechain.org** (e-mail scams and chain letters) or **www.darwinawards.com** (weird accidents) to find something that simply tickles your fancy, then comment on it.

At **www.newsisfree.com/newsmap**, the colour-coded map views of world news stories are a great way of putting yourself in touch with the current buzz.

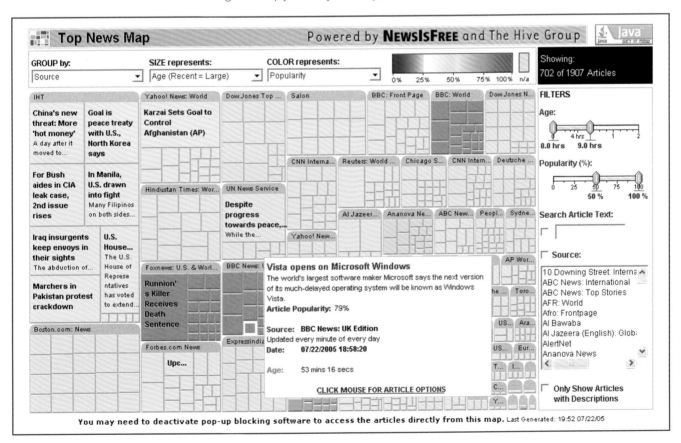

PART **4**

Building a blog

PART **4**

Basic blogging

In this workshop we'll build a simple but attractive weblog (or "blog") using the excellent WordPress.com. The service is free and includes everything you need to post your words online – and you can be up and running in a matter of minutes.

In the first edition of this book we used the free Blogger.com but, incredibly, it's barely been updated since then – whereas Wordpress.com gets better and better. As we'll discover in this tutorial you can choose from a range of professionally created designs that will give your blog real impact, you can use all kinds of attractive text formatting and you can even enable visitors to leave comments.

It may be easy to use, but WordPress is far from basic – and that's what we like about it. It's simple enough for absolute beginners to use but powerful enough for even the most demanding web publishers, and the whole thing runs in your web browser.

So what are we waiting for? Let's build a blog!

1

All you need to use WordPress.com is a web browser and an internet connection. It doesn't really matter which browser you use – we've updated WordPress blogs using the horrible wee browsers you find in mobile phones – but for this tutorial we'll stick with internet Explorer. The first step is to visit **www.wordpress.com** *to start the sign-up process.*

To build a blog, you'll need to choose a username. It's a good idea to think about this, because the username will become part of your web address. You'll also need to enter a password and give WordPress your email address so that the site can contact you.

WordPress takes security seriously, and if you enter a password it thinks is too simple (which means it's really easy for other people to guess) then you'll see lots of bright pink boxes as WordPress asks you to choose a better password.

Once WordPress is happy with your password you can see the suggested domain name, which will be in the format username.wordpress.com. This will be your blog's web address, and you can change it if you wish. You can also give your blog a title. The more descriptive, the better.

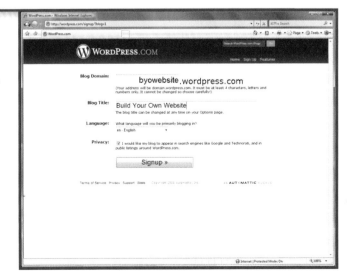

WordPress will now send you an email to confirm your account, and you won't be able to do much until the email arrives. It usually appears within a few seconds. The email contains a web link; click on the link and you should see the "Your account is now active" screen. Click on Login to continue.

From: WordPress.com <donotreply@wordpress.com>
Subject: **Activate byowebsite.wordpress.com**
Date: 29 June 2008 11:35:22 BST
To: Gary Marshall

Howdy,

Thank you for signing up with WordPress.com. You are one step away from blogging at byowebsite.wordpress.com. Please click this link to activate your blog:

http://wordpress.com/activate/0fe8fd85bc044854

--The WordPress.com Team

The WordPress login screen will now appear. Enter your username and password and click on the Log In button to continue. Only tick the Remember Me button if your computer isn't used by anybody else, or it means anybody will be able to get their grubby hands on your blog!

This is the WordPress dashboard, and you'll be seeing a lot of it – it's a one-stop shop for all your blogging needs, from changing the design to adding new content or keeping an eye on visitors' comments. Let's start by making our blog look good. To do this, click on the blue Design link at the top of the screen.

You should now see the Design section of the dashboard, with a selection of themes displayed at the bottom of the screen. To see a bigger version of a particular theme, click on it and you'll see a much bigger preview; to apply it to your blog, click on the Activate link to the top-right of the preview.

Once you've activated a theme you'll return to the Design section of your dashboard, and the image under Current Theme should now reflect the theme you've just chosen. If you look immediately to the right of your blog title you'll see a box labelled Visit Site. Click on it to see your new blog in all its glory.

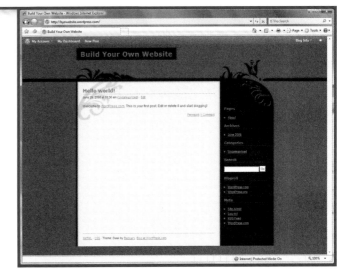

This is almost exactly what visitors will see when they visit your blog – the only difference is the grey WordPress toolbar at the very top of the window, which is there for you to continue working on your blog. As you can see the blog looks good, but it's rather empty. Time to add some content. Click on the My Dashboard link to return to the dashboard.

In the orange bar you'll see two big buttons: Write a New Page and Write a New Post. Although both buttons enable you to add content to your blog, they work in slightly different ways. Let's take a short break to explain the difference.

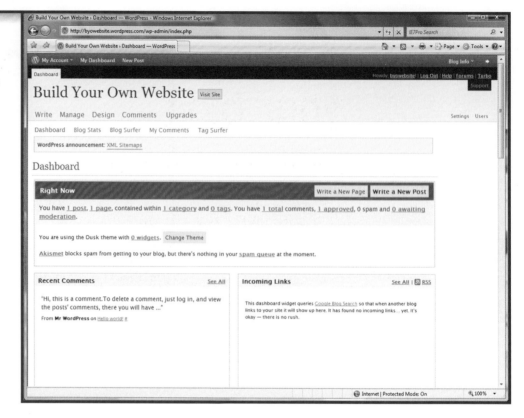

Posts versus pages

A traditional blog is made up of "posts", which are similar to newspaper articles, and your blog front page will usually show the most recent posts with the newest one at the top. That's great, because it means visitors always see the last thing you've published, but it means that as you add more posts, the older ones disappear from the front page.

When a post disappears from the front page of your blog, it remains accessible in two ways. There's an "older posts" link at the foot of your blog, and there are archive links that enable visitors to see everything you posted on a specific day or between two dates. But what happens if there's something you want your visitors to be able to find quickly, such as your biography, online CV or contact information? Say hello to pages. With WordPress, pages appear as buttons or links on your front page, which means they're only ever a click away.

So which should you use? For day-to-day blogging, use posts; for information or content you want to highlight, use pages.

BUILDING A BLOG

PART 4

Adding content to your blog

Now that we know the difference between posts and pages, let's start putting some content into our blog. If you look at the WordPress dashboard you'll see that your blog already has 1 post and 1 page, so let's take a look. Click on the link that says "You have 1 post".

This is the Manage Posts screen, which makes it easy to see what you've published on your blog. As you can see, we already have one post called "Hello World!". Click on the Hello World link to see it.

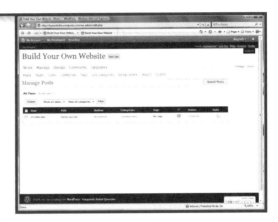

WordPress will now take you to the Write Post screen. You'll see this every time you create a new post or edit an existing one. As you can see, it's nice and straightforward: there's a prominent title box which displays the post title and there's a word-processor-style box where you do your actual editing. Let's replace the title with something more interesting.

To change the title, it's just a matter of highlighting the text that's already in there and replacing it with the text you want to use. The same applies to the text in the main editing box, so let's change that as well.

4 Once again it's just a matter of highlighting the text you want to get rid of and then typing your own text. If you wish, you can use the word-processor-style icons to make bits of text bold or italic, or to create a list of bullet points. There are some extra buttons too. Let's find out what they do.

5 When you blog, you'll often use somebody else's words; WordPress has a special way of formatting that so it's immediately obvious when you're quoting. Simply click on the text that you've quoted from elsewhere and click the Blockquote icon, which is the button with the two curly quote marks on it. You'll see that the text you selected has now become indented on screen.

6 You can also use the toolbar to add a link, which is very good manners if you're referring to somebody else's blog. To make a link, simply highlight the text you want to turn into a link and then click the Insert/Edit Link button (it looks like a little chain). This displays the Insert/Edit Link dialog; simply enter the web address in the Link URL and click on Insert.

7 As you can see, the text has become a link with blue, underlined text. Let's see how this will appear to our visitors. Click on the Save button at the right of the window.

At first it seems as if nothing's changed, but if you look towards the top of the screen you'll see a yellow bar explaining that your post has been updated. That means your post has been published and is available for anybody on the internet to see. Let's take a look. Click on View This Post to continue.

Your blog will now open in a new window, and you'll see that both your quote and your link are really quite obvious (exactly how they appear depends on the template you've chosen). You'll also see that there's a comment underneath the post. In this case it's an automatically generated one, but over time you'll start getting comments from real people – although you can disable comments altogether if you'd rather not get comments from your visitors.

Publish and be damned?

A blog without comments is like a pub without alcohol: it's perfectly pleasant, but it's lacking something important. You'll find that in most cases the people who comment on your blog are perfectly decent, intelligent, interesting and funny people, and the conversations you have with them are a pleasure. Unfortunately, like everything else on the internet, there is a small minority of people that try to ruin things for everyone.

There are two kinds of commenters to watch out for: spammers and abusive commenters. Spammers will post comments that have no purpose other than to link to their own website, and they're a pain at best and a downright menace at worst.

We've had spammers leave comments that have no content other than dozens of links to extremely dodgy websites. Why do they do it? Because search engines rank websites on the basis of the number of sites that link to them, the spammers are trying to boost their Google ranking. The fact that it doesn't work doesn't stop them from doing it. Luckily it's easy to deal with them, because you can delete unwanted comments from your WordPress dashboard.

Abusive commenters are trickier. Blogging purists say you should never delete any comment, no matter how abusive, but such comments can ruin your blog's atmosphere, dissuade nicer people from posting and offend anybody who happens to read them. We think the best approach is to create a set of "house rules" for your blog, so for example you might tell commenters that abusive posts will be deleted. If your rules are fair and applied consistently, then regular readers won't complain.

PART

Better blogging

The more you can do on the internet, the more you want to do – and blogging is no exception. We've already discovered how to publish text using WordPress.com, and in this workshop we'll get stuck into some of the more advanced features such as including images, embedding YouTube clips, dealing with comments and adding cool features using Widgets.

Although some of the things we'll cover are quite advanced, don't worry: everything we're going to look at is very simple to use, and even the most powerful options only require a few mouse clicks.

Log in to your Wordpress.com account if you haven't done so already and click on Write a New Post. As before, simply give your post a title and enter your post text in the main editing section.

Click on Add Media and you should see the screen shown here. You have two choices here: you can link to an image on another website or you can upload one from your hard disk. We'll go for the latter option, so click on the Choose Files To Upload button.

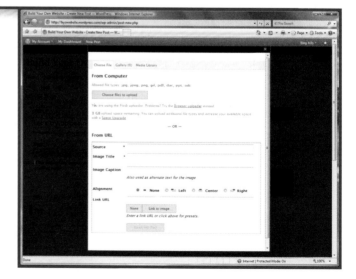

3

You'll now see the standard file browser. Simply navigate to the folder where you've stored your images, select the one you'd like to upload and then click on the Open button.

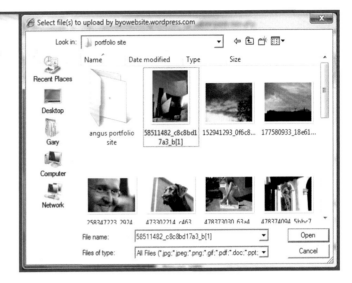

4

After a few seconds you should now see a thumbnail image and some fields. You should always give your images a title and a caption, particularly when – as here – the original filename is pretty much meaningless.

5

There are two other options here: Alignment and Size. The former specifies how the image should appear on your blog. None simply inserts it in the post, while Left, Center and Right flow the text around it. Unless you have extremely large images, you should select Full Size. Click on Insert Into Post when you've made your choice.

6

Wordpress will now return to the Write Post screen, and you should see your image in the actual post. In this example we've chosen Left alignment, so our image is at the left of the post and our text sits immediately to the right of it. Click on Preview This Post to see what it will look like.

7

Eek! Our image is far too big. No problem: just return to the Write Post screen, click on the image and then resize it to something more sensible. Once again, click on Preview This Post when you've done this.

8

That's much better. Once you're happy with the way your post looks, close the preview window and return to the Write Post screen. Click on Publish and your new post will now be available on the internet for anybody to see.

Now, let's try some video. We'll embed a YouTube video clip, so the first step is to visit YouTube and find a clip you like. Once you've done this, copy the page address from your web browser's address bar – that is, the bit beginning **http://www.youtube.com/**. Close the window and return to WordPress when you've done this.

In the toolbar above your post's text, click on the Add Video icon – it's the one that looks like a movie frame. The Add Video screen should now appear. This time we'll ignore the Choose Files To Upload button and look at the From URL field instead.

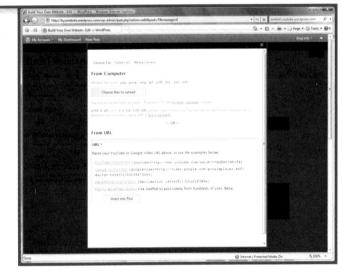

Right-click in the URL field and select Paste. This should paste the web address of your chosen YouTube clip in the appropriate space. Click on the Insert Into Post button when you've done this.

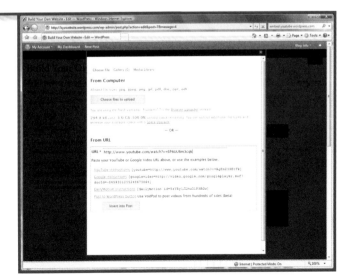

You should now see a line beginning "[youtube=" in your post. That's good, because that's the code WordPress.com uses to include YouTube videos. The clip itself won't appear in the editing window; to see it, you'll need to click on Publish and then on the Visit Site button towards the top of the screen.

And here's the result: one embedded YouTube clip. It's a particularly easy way of getting your own movies onto your blog: simply sign up for a (free) YouTube account, click on Videos and then click on the Upload button.

As you can see, the upload screen is nice and straightforward, asking you to give your clip a title and description. Once you've entered the relevant information it's just a matter of clicking Upload Video to choose a video clip from your hard disk, or Use Quick Capture to make an instant video from your PC's webcam (assuming you have one, of course). You'll find that many mobile phones enable you to upload videos to YouTube too.

Using categories

It won't take long before your blog is positively packed with posts, but that has a downside because it can make your blog very difficult to navigate. Using categories can make a big difference: if you assign a category to each post, visitors can then click on the particular category that interests them rather than wade through weeks, months or even years of posts.

In the WordPress Dashboard, click on the Manage link towards the top of the screen. This takes you to the Manage section, where you can easily organise your blog. The default view, shown here, is a list of all the posts you've made – and you'll see that you can filter the posts by date or by category. So let's add some categories to our blog.

Click on the Categories link – it's the fourth link from the left. You should now see a single category, "uncategorized". Let's change that. In the Add Category section, type an appropriate category in the Category Name field. You can add a description too if you like. Click on Add Category when you're finished.

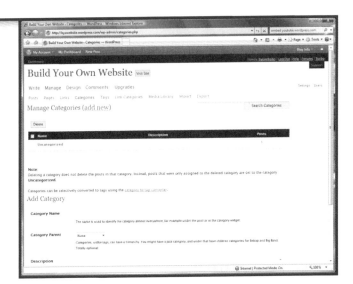

3

Repeat the process for as many categories as you'd like to add. Each time you click on Add Category, you'll see your new category appear in the list at the top of the screen. As the list gets bigger, you'll probably need to scroll down to see the Add Category section.

4

You can have categories within categories, so for example under Photography you might have personal photos, arty photos, buildings and so on. To add sub-categories, type the name of your new category as normal but this time, click on the Category Parent drop-down. Choose the appropriate category and then click on Add Category.

5

This time, our new category looks slightly different: it says "Photos – Buildings" – that is, Buildings is a sub-category within our Photos category. You can have further sub-categories so, for example, you might have Photos > Buildings > Interiors or Photos > Buildings > Tourist Attractions. It's entirely up to you.

To use categories, simply create a blog post as normal – but before you publish it, scroll down the screen until you see the Categories box. Click on All Categories and you'll see a list of available categories. To apply one or more categories to your post, simply check the box next to the appropriate category or categories.

Once you start using categories, you'll see two changes on your blog: beneath each post title you'll see the categories that apply to that post, and in your blog's navigation bar you'll see links for each category used in your blog. Categories you've created but not used yet won't appear. If your visitors click on a category name they'll see all posts in that category.

You can use categories too: in the WordPress Dashboard, if you click on Manage you can filter your posts so you only see the ones in a particular category. It's a huge time saver when you're trying to find something you've written in the past.

Expanding your blog with widgets

As we've seen, a WordPress blog is pretty impressive – but you can add even more features using widgets. Widgets are little add-ons that plug into your blog and add new features. For example, you can use the Flickr Widget to display photos from your Flickr account, or the Calendar Widget to let your visitors search your posts by date. Adding widgets couldn't be easier – and they don't cost a penny.

To use widgets, go to the WordPress Dashboard and click on Design > Widgets. You should now see the screen shown here, with a big list of available widgets. Let's add something useful – a Search box. To do this, click on the Add link next to the Search option.

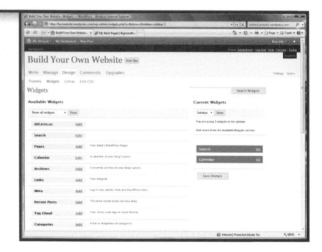

You'll now see a blue box marked Search at the right of the screen. Let's add something else – the Calendar widget. This will now appear below the Search box at the right of the screen. To change the order, simply drag the boxes around. Click Save Changes when you've done this.

Click on Visit Site to see your widgets in action. As you can see, we now have a search box at the top right of our blog and a calendar immediately below it. You'll also see that all the other things that used to appear in the right-hand panel have disappeared. That's because when you add widgets, they replace the default options (categories and so on). That's easy to sort. Back to the Widgets page!

To add more content, just add more widgets. Here we've gone for Archives, Recent Posts, Recent Comments and Categories, which is more than enough to be getting on with. We've then changed the order by dragging and dropping the blue boxes around. Remember to click on Save Changes when you've added new widgets or they won't appear on your blog.

And here's the result: our sidebar starts off with a calendar, then there's a list of recent posts, recent comments, categories and archives. Last but not least we've given our visitors a search box so they can easily find anything they're looking for – which will come in handy when we've been ranting about all kinds of things for months on end.

WordPress.com has another trick up its sleeve: it can tell you who's looking at your site, what they're looking at and where they came from. In the Dashboard, click on Blog Stats and you'll see the screen shown here. As we've just created our blog there's no information here as yet, but over time the Blog Stats screen provides a wealth of information including:

● Referrers – this tells you what links people clicked to arrive at your blog, so for example if another blogger has linked to you, you'll see the address of their page here.
● Top posts and pages – as the title suggests, this tells you which parts of your blog have attracted the most visitors.
● Search engine terms – this is one of the most useful bits of information, because it tells you what people were searching for when they found your blog.
● Clicks – what links in your blog your visitors clicked on, taking them away from your blog.

Together these bits of information are enormously useful, particularly if you're trying to achieve something – such as making money – from your blog. Knowledge is power.

PART  # Even better blogging

So far we've concentrated on the sort of things any blogger will want to do – creating posts, making it easy for visitors to find content, adding images and video – but blogs can do more than just provide a platform for your thoughts. Some bloggers have ended up with lucrative book deals, others make money from their posts, and still others are involved in "podcasting" – a kind of internet-age radio. Could your blog make you rich, famous or both?

Blogging for bucks

One of the most common questions people ask about blogging is whether you can make money from it. The answer is yes – to a point. Unless you attract a massive audience (and by massive we mean millions of readers), you probably shouldn't put down a deposit on an Aston Martin, but that doesn't mean you can't generate a bit of cash. Blogs typically make money for their owners in four ways: through commission, through selling ads, through good old-fashioned begging and through spin-offs. Let's look at each one in turn.

Making money from commission schemes

Commission schemes – also known as affiliate schemes – are very simple. When you sign up, you'll be given a referrer code and if you link to products using that code you'll get a cut of any resulting sales. Some of the web's biggest names run such schemes, so for example Amazon.co.uk has an affiliate scheme called Associates (**http://affiliate-program-amazon.co.uk/gp/associates/join/main.html**). It sounds great, too: once your application has been accepted (Amazon, like most retailers, doesn't want to be associated with any dodgy sites) you get up to 10% commission on any sale that came from your website.

Other schemes could be even more lucrative. Affiliate Window (**www.affiliatewindow.com**) deals with big names such as Currys, John Lewis and Marks & Spencer; while it costs £5 to sign up, the commission rates are excellent.

The downside to all of this? You can't simply stick a bunch of links on your website and expect millions of people to click on them. For a commission scheme to work, the retailers you choose need to be relevant to your website – there's not much point in advertising flat-screen TVs if your blog is about being broke – and you need your visitors not just to click on the link, but to actually buy something. More often than not, people who sign up to such schemes expecting to make a fortune end up bitterly disappointed.

That doesn't mean such schemes aren't worth considering, though. For example, if your blog is reviewing music or movies then links to the CD or DVD you've just reviewed could well result in sales – provided the retailer you're linking to offers them

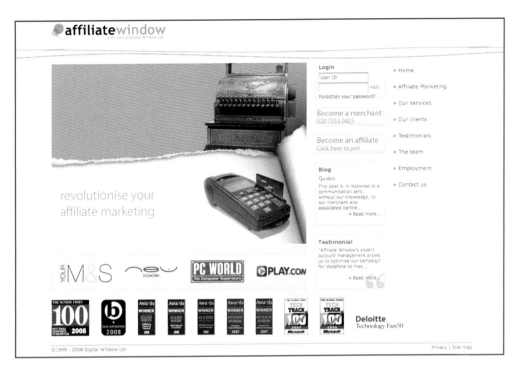

Affiliate schemes offer you a cut of any purchases your visitors make, but it's important to choose your offers wisely. People visiting a blog about being broke probably aren't going to buy giant flat-screen TVs.

at a decent price, of course. However, affiliate marketing isn't a get-rich-quick system: you'll need to invest a lot of time and effort to generate any significant sums.

Making money from adverts

Many blogs include little Google adverts, and if their visitors click on the links the site owner makes money. Signing up is free (**http://adsense.google.com**) and the site generates the necessary code for you to copy and paste into your blog.

Once again, it's not a lot of money – we know of a blog that gets a few thousand daily visitors and generates about £50 every three months in ads – but over time it could still generate a tidy sum, particularly if you're blogging about a niche subject. One enterprising blogger created a blog about the asbestos industry, not because he was particularly interested in asbestos but because he did his homework and discovered that nobody else was blogging about it. He knew that the more specific your subject matter, the more advertising revenue you can expect; if everybody's writing about the subject you're covering, advertising rates will be very, very low.

It's worth noting that many free blogging services – including WordPress.com – don't let you put such adverts on your blog, which is fair enough. After all, why should they give you a service for free if you're going to use it to make money without giving them any? The big exception to this is the free Blogger.com service, which is owned by Google and which couldn't be happier if you plaster your posts with Google adverts.

If you do decide to run adverts (or take part in an affiliate scheme) it's very important to be transparent. Blog readers tend to get angry if they feel a site is doing sneaky marketing instead of being honest, and a site that simply tries to sell people stuff isn't likely to attract a huge audience – which is why we don't think you should bother with "get paid to blog" services, which get you to blog about specific things in return for cash. The

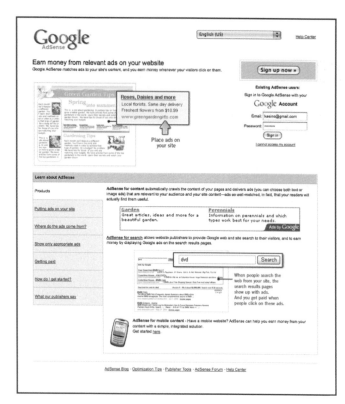

Google's AdSense enables you to run little adverts on your blog, but you'll find that free blogging services – with the exception of Blogger.com – won't let you use it.

Some blogs, such as the satirical Stuff White People Like, have resulted in book deals for their creators.

returns are tiny, the subjects are usually rather dull and the list of Excluded Domains – that is, web addresses that aren't eligible – tends to rule out all the free blogging platforms.

Making money from begging

Some bloggers have a "donate now" button on their blogs, usually via the PayPal money transfer service; others publish their Amazon.co.uk wish lists in the hope that grateful readers will buy them things. Sometimes it works, although more often than not it doesn't. Unless you're providing a fantastic public service for free, you've amassed an exceptionally loyal readership or you're young, good-looking and don't find anything really weird and creepy about strangers offering gifts, it's unlikely that simply asking for things will make your fortune.

Making money from spin-offs

You might not make any money from your blog, but your blog could help you make money in other ways. Fancy being a published author? The satirical "Stuff White People Like" blog resulted in a book deal worth a reported £150,000 in 2008, and various other bloggers have turned their blogs into proper books on everything from sex lives to the reality of working for the NHS. However, despite the publicity, the reality of such book deals often falls short: Gawker.com, one of the world's most popular weblogs, sold fewer than 1000 copies of its spin-off book "The Gawker Guide to Conquering All Media", while the UK's biggest blog-to-book publisher went bust in early 2008 after incurring massive losses. As a result, book publishers are considerably more cautious about blogs, even popular ones: they do still look to blogs for potential new titles, but you'll need to attract a huge audience to get their attention.

There are other ways you can benefit from blogging, though. If you blog about your skills or hobbies, it can boost your profile and perhaps result in paid work – for example, photographers who blog can find readers contacting them with offers of work, while blogs by experts in specific fields can attract the attention of TV and radio producers or newspaper editors. And sometimes blogging can become paid blogging: some of the world's biggest blogs, such as technology blog Engadget, frequently advertise paid writing positions where your existing blog acts as your CV.

There's another way in which your blog can become something more interesting: if you podcast or videocast, you can turn your blog into an online radio station or TV channel.

PART

BUILDING A BLOG

Radio heads

Fancy running your own radio station or starring in your own TV show? With podcasting and videocasting you can – and you can do it from your blog.

A podcast is a blog post that uses audio instead of text and a videocast is the same but with video. Putting one together couldn't be easier: simply record your audio or video, save the file and stick it on the internet. (You'll need your own web space to do this with audio files, but you can use YouTube for video – and we'd strongly recommend doing so, because video files are massive and you'll need a lot of web space.)

Creating a podcast couldn't be simpler. Here's how to do it.

● Record your audio – free software such as Audacity (**http://audacity.sourceforge.net**) is perfect for this.
● Save the file as an MP3.
● Upload the MP3 to your web space.
● Create a new blog post and use the Add Audio link in WordPress to link to the MP3.

And that's it – although there's an optional fifth step, which is to submit your podcasts to a directory such as Podcast Blaster (**www.podcastblaster.com**) or to Apple's iTunes (**www.apple.com/support/itunes/store/podcast**). The latter option can take a few weeks (and you need to install the free iTunes software to submit your podcast in the first place), but it's worth doing if you want to reach the widest possible audience.

Linking to an audio clip in WordPress is nice and straightforward: just click the Add Audio link and tell WordPress where to find the file.

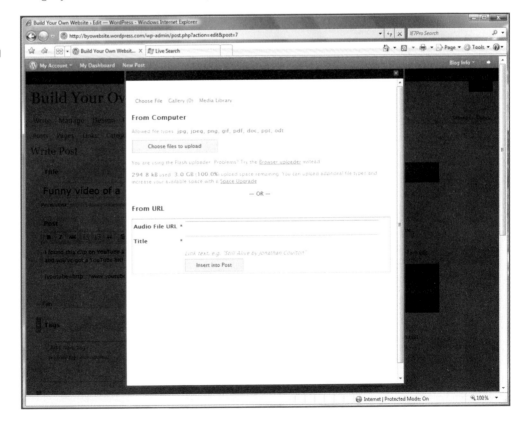

There are two things you need to consider before podcasting, or three if you include deciding what you want to talk about. The first is music and the second is bandwidth. Getting either one wrong could be expensive, so it's important to know the potential dangers.

It's illegal to use people's music without permission, so while it's tempting to put your favourite songs in the background to your podcast it could result in a hefty fine. Unless you're dealing with unsigned musicians – that is, artists who make music but aren't signed to a record company – you'll need a license from the Mechanical Copyright Protection Society (**www.mcps.co.uk**), which will cost you a few hundred pounds per year. One way to get around this is to get in touch with unsigned bands, who will often be delighted with the attention and who won't charge you a penny. Alternatively, visit **www.podsafeaudio.com** to find music by artists who are quite happy for you to use their music, without payment, in your podcast.

Bandwidth means data transfer – that is, how many megabytes of data your web space can handle in a given time. Audio files are big and video files bigger still, so while 1MB of data is enough for thousands of pages of text, it's around 60 seconds of music. If your web host has a limit on how much data you can transfer each month (most do), too many downloads could result in a big bill. For example, at the time of writing, 1&1 internet's basic web hosting package gives you 3GB of data transfer per month, which is enough for just under 1000 three-minute MP3 files – so if your podcast is half an hour long, more than a few hundred downloads will crack the monthly limit.

To avoid this, don't save your MP3s at the highest possible sound quality. There's no point making your audio files any bigger than they need to be. Experiment with different settings to get the best trade-off between sound quality and file size and avoid music if you don't need to use it – speech is perfectly legible at much lower quality settings than you can get away with when you're using music. We've found that a quality of 160Kbps is fine for music podcasts, while 128Kbps is perfectly acceptable for speech.

It's also a very good idea to keep tabs on your web space statistics. Most commercial web space includes a control panel that tells you all kinds of useful information, and you can keep an eye on your data transfer to see whether you're approaching the monthly limit. If you are, you can do two things: you can shell out some money for a more generous web hosting package or you can temporarily remove the audio files until the following month.

What about video? After all, video files are much, much bigger than MP3s. We think we've found a brilliant solution: make your own YouTube channel. That way YouTube does all the work, stores all your files and handles all the downloads, and it's free whether you get one download a month or 100,000. With YouTube, if you become an internet celebrity you don't need to worry about data transfer limits and bandwidth bills. We'll discover how to create a YouTube channel on the next page.

I want my MP3s

Audio software can create all kinds of files: MP3, Windows Media, AAC and weirdly named formats such as Ogg Vorbis. We think you should stick to MP3, though. It might not be the most technologically advanced audio file format – AAC and Windows Media can create slightly smaller files than MP3 can manage – but it has one important trick up its sleeve: it works on almost anything. Some MP3 players and computer music programs can play Windows Media but not AAC, or they might play AAC but not Windows Media, but they all play MP3 – as do many phones, car stereos and other gadgets. By using MP3s for your podcasts you can be sure that you're reaching the widest possible audience.

PART 4 You're watching Channel Me

In our last workshop we discovered how to upload videos to YouTube; now we're going to take things a step further and create our own video channel. To do this, you'll need to sign up for a free YouTube account if you haven't done so already.

As soon as you upload a video to YouTube, the site automatically creates a channel for you. To see it, go to **www.youtube.com/user/username**, *where username is the name YouTube knows you by. For example, to see our channel, you visit* **www.youtube.com/user/kasino72**.

It's easy to edit your channel: just click on the cunningly named Edit Channel button and you'll see this screen, which enables you to control what happens on your channel – so you can disable comments or limit them to friends, or change your channel type from YouTuber (the default) to Director, Musician, Comedian, Guru or Reporter.

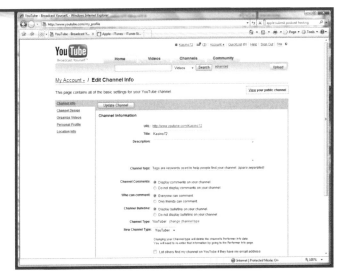

3

Click on Channel Design to change the way your channel looks. On this screen you can specify a colour scheme, what content should appear on the page and where key information, such as your videos list, should appear. Click on Update Channel when you're finished.

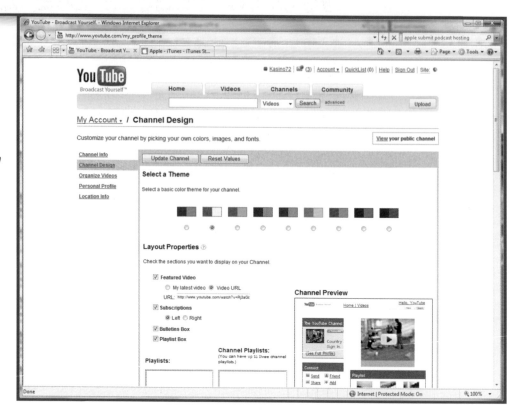

4

As you can see, when you create your own YouTube channel you're in good company: bands such as Radiohead, comedians, directors and charities all have their own YouTube channels. We think this is one of the best ways to videocast, especially if you don't want to pay for web space. And remember, you can embed the videos in your blog, as we saw in our last workshop.

WordPress's big brother

For all its joys, there are some things WordPress.com can't do. You can't display ads, there's a limit to how much space you get, there are only a few templates to choose from and the choice of Widgets and other extras is fairly limited. If you like WordPress but wish it was even more powerful, we'd recommend . . . WordPress!

Don't worry, we haven't lost our minds. There are two versions of WordPress. The one we've used so far, WordPress.com, is best for blogging beginners but if you need more power then WordPress.org will be right up your street. Like WordPress.com, it's completely free but unlike the .com version it doesn't include web space. Free web space – such as the space offered by firms such as Tripod – isn't up to the job, but almost all paid-for packages will include everything you need to run WordPress on your own web space.

Why you should consider WordPress.org

Although at first glance it looks almost identical to the WordPress.com system, WordPress.org is much more powerful. That's why it's used by organisations including the *New York Times*, Sony and thousands of professional bloggers. It isn't particularly difficult to set up and it's incredibly expandable: there are stacks of websites offering free templates to make your blog look great, and there are hundreds of plugins that add even more features. It's an excellent blogging system, and you can also use it to create complex websites by using Pages instead of Posts.

What you need to install WordPress on your own web space

First of all, you'll need some web space – but there are specific things that WordPress needs to function. The system requirements are PHP version 4.3 or greater and MySQL version 4.0 or later. These are features most paid-for web space provides as standard – PHP is a programming language and MySQL is a kind of database, and many sites use them – but it's important to check first. Most web-hosting companies provide this information in their "features" sales blurb but, if not, WordPress provides a standard letter you can send them:

```
    I'm interested in running the open-source
WordPress <http://wordpress.org/> blogging
software and I was wondering if my account
supported the following:
  * PHP 4.3 or greater
  * MySQL 4.0 or greater
  * The mod_rewrite Apache module
  Thanks!
```

You don't need to know what any of that actually means; all you need is a "yes" from your web-space provider. Once you've got that, you're ready to go. Download the software from

http://wordpress.org/download – it's free – and make sure you've got your web space username and passwords handy. In particular, you'll need the FTP username and password that your web space provider has given you.

To upload WordPress, you'll need an FTP (File Transfer Protocol) program. If you don't already have one, we'd recommend the excellent – and free – FileZilla from **http://filezilla-project.org**.

The next step is to install WordPress; the whole process takes about five minutes. There are two ways to do this: you can follow the step-by-step instructions at **http://codex.wordpress.org/Installing_WordPress** or you can contact the wonderful people at Install4Free (**http://install4free.wordpress.net**). Install4Free is run by a team of WordPress evangelists who really, really like the software and want everybody to use it; they will happily set up WordPress for you – for free. There are three important caveats, though. The first is that the service is strictly for personal blogs, so companies aren't eligible; the second is that the service isn't immediate, so you might have to wait a few days for somebody to do it; and the third is that from time to time, the nice people at Install4free are simply overwhelmed with the demand for their services and can't take on any new assignments. If that's the case when you visit, we'd suggest trying it yourself: the instructions on WordPress.org are really very good and the process is much less scary than it might appear.

Which WordPress is best for you?

Our table shows the most important differences between WordPress.com and WordPress.org.

	WordPress.com	WordPress.org
Cost	Free	Free
Web address	yourname.wordpress.com	Your own domain name
Web space	Included	Not included
Will it work on free web space?	n/a	Probably not
Storage space	3GB (more available for a fee)	Only limited by your hosting package
Installation	Already installed	Do it yourself
Backups and maintenance	Automatic	Do it yourself
Software upgrades and patches	Automatic	Do it yourself (automated plugin also available)
Available themes	Just a few	Hundreds
Can you edit the themes?	No*	Yes
Sidebar Widgets	Yes	Yes
Expandable via plugins	No	Yes
Anti-spam technology	Built-in	Via plugin
Blog statistics	Built-in	Via plugin
Smartphone support	Yes**	Yes**
Create posts by email	No	Yes
Can you run ads?	No	Yes
Members-only blogs?	Yes	Yes
Multi-user blogs	Yes	Yes
Do I need any technical knowledge?	No	A little (for installation and maintenance)

*   Custom CSS enables you to use your own style sheet, but it's a paid-for add-on.
** Requires a mobile phone with a web browser.

If you're not sure which version is best for you, don't worry: if you start off with WordPress.com and decide at a later point that you'd really like to use WordPress.org on your own web space, it's easy to export your blog from WordPress.com to your own web space.

In most cases WordPress takes about five minutes to install and the instructions on the WordPress.org website make the process nice and straightforward. It's not as scary as it looks.

If you're not confident about installing WordPress yourself, the nice people at Install4Free will do it for you – provided it's for a personal blog and not a business one.

One of the best things about WordPress.org is the sheer range of goodies you can get for free – including professional-looking templates that make your blog look brilliant. You'll find them at **http://themes.wordpress.net**.

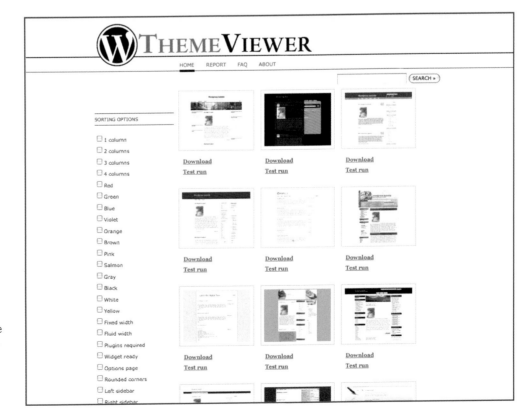

5

PART 5

BUILD YOUR OWN WEBSITE

Writing your own web pages

PART 5 The ABC of HTML

In this section we're going to tackle how to write the code for a web page by hand. The idea of writing code might seem a little daunting at first, like learning a secret language spoken only by geeks. However, creating a web page from scratch is not as complicated as it may seem, and it helps enormously to understand what's going on behind the scenes when your web design skills improve and you want to move beyond the confines of a WYSIWYG editor (see p.23). To create a web page, all you need is a web browser and a basic text editor such as Windows Notepad (which comes with every version of Windows) or TextEdit on a Mac.

Simple coding

Most web pages are written using a language called HTML, which stands for HyperText Markup Language. It's simpler than it sounds:

● The word "hypertext" refers to the fact that you can move around between pages on the web using *links*. Links are the words and images you can click on to get taken from one page to another or to jump around within a page. This ability to move around the web using these links is what makes it "hyper" text as opposed to regular text

● "Markup language" refers to the code, or markup, which you add to plain text on your web page in order to control how it is displayed and structured.

Coding a web page is similar to the process of adding formatting to a word-processing document. For example, consider a document in Microsoft Word. Here we can see several styles of text in the drop down menu.

The difference when creating a web page is that rather than adding styles using menus in a word processor, you add things called "tags" into the text itself. These tags are then read by the viewer's web browser, at which point the browser knows how to display the document onscreen. In other words, a web page's overall appearance is determined by the user's software, which makes it all the more critical that the web designer and the browser speak the same language. If there are mistakes or omissions in the markup, strange things happen.

Marking up a document is akin to adding styles to a document, as you might do in Microsoft Word.

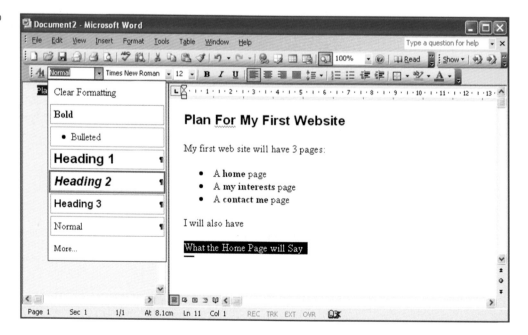

Let's dive in for just a moment. Here we can see an example of a very basic web page in Windows Notepad. Don't worry if it looks complicated at first, as all will become clear very quickly:

You can write a web page in something as basic as Windows Notepad.

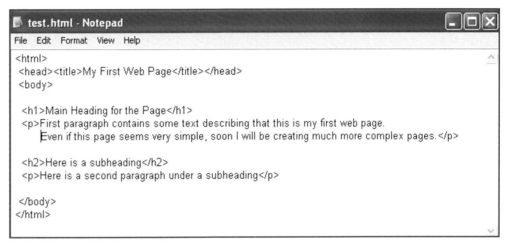

To start with, just focus on the bits from the fifth line down. The main heading is written between tags which say <h1> and </h1>. These tags indicate that anything in between them should be a level 1 heading. The subheading is inside tags that say <h2> and </h2>, indicating that anything between them should be a level 2 heading. And the paragraphs are inside tags that say <p> and </p>, thus marking the start and end of the paragraph. Note that an opening tag contains a coded instruction and a closing tag mimics it but includes a forward slash. This slash tells the browser to stop applying the tag's instructions at that point. Every opening tag must – well, certainly should – have a corresponding closing tag.

Here we can see what this page looks like in Internet Explorer.

Browsers automatically format some elements in different ways.

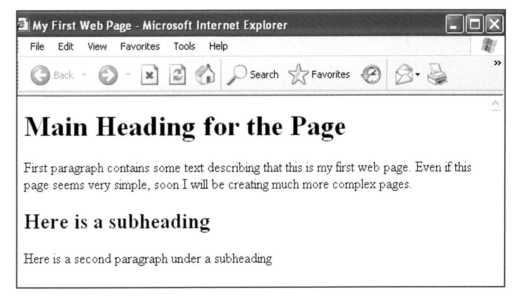

So, when creating a web page you add tags to control the appearance of the page much as you would apply formatting to a Word document. However, rather than focusing on *styling* the document, which is what you do when formatting a word processed document, you need to think about the *structure* of the page.

A web page should describe its structure

While the example of a web page which you just saw was very basic, it does illustrate an important point: the markup in a web page should describe the structure of that page.

If you think about books for a moment, they tend to follow a structure that is loosely based around these lines:

A title that refers to the whole book
    A table of contents
    One or more chapters
        Each chapter has its own title or heading
        Under each chapter heading are often several sub headings
        Inside the sub headings are paragraphs, images, possibly some lists of bullet points, and so on
    An index

The primary purpose of markup language is to describe the structure of a document in order that any web browser can display it correctly.

A brief history of HTML

Let's now backtrack briefly. When the web first came out it was quite a grey, dull place. There was little colour and images were rare. Its main purpose was to facilitate the easy exchange and retrieval of academic work to help researchers find information that might help them with their work and save them replicating studies unnecessarily.

However, as the web grew, all manner of people began to see personal and commercial potential for it. They started creating their own web pages to build online communities and to advertise companies and products. People wanted to be able to control the way that their web pages looked when viewed on a browser, and quite naturally they expected the same level of control as designers who create print publications. A web page should look just the same on computer A and computer B, quite regardless of whether one is a PC and the other is a Mac and one is running a particular web browser, like Microsoft Internet Explorer, and the other something quite different, like Netscape Navigator (as was).

As the desire and eventually the need to develop web pages increased, HTML expanded to not only describe the structure of documents but also to control their presentation: how pages looked, the colours used, the size of fonts, and so on.

All these new markup possibilities made web pages far more attractive. However, it also meant that web pages were designed to work only with desktop computers on which screens were roughly the same size. As the internet has evolved, people no longer just want to access the web via their desktop computers. They also want to be able to get information on their mobile phones, TV set-top boxes, handheld organisers, and all manner of other devices. The problem is that a web page controlled solely by HTML can look fantastic on a desktop monitor but be completely useless on a smaller screen.

As a consequence, web page authors are now strongly encouraged not to use markup language to control how their documents look. Rather, markup should describe the structure of a document, such as what is a heading and what is a paragraph. This doesn't mean that web pages have to be boring. Quite the contrary, in fact: we now have a better tool to style our web pages, the language of cascading style sheets, which we'll meet later in this book.

Cascading style sheets (or CSS) have several advantages over HTML, notably that you can create different style rules for different types of devices. This ensures that the same page can be displayed properly on just about anything from a widescreen plasma display to a mobile phone. We will see other advantages of CSS when we meet it later.

The same web page on a desktop PC and a mobile phone.

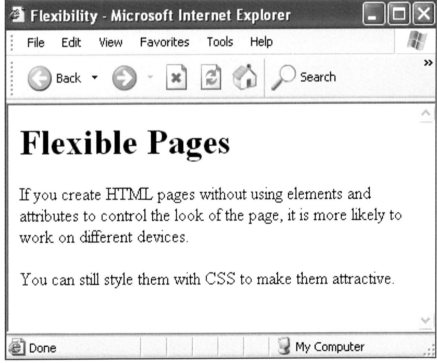

The difference between tags, elements and attributes

One thing that really helps with writing web pages is understanding the difference between tags, elements and attributes. Consider the following diagram:

Most elements are made up of an opening tag, a closing tag, and the content between the two tags.

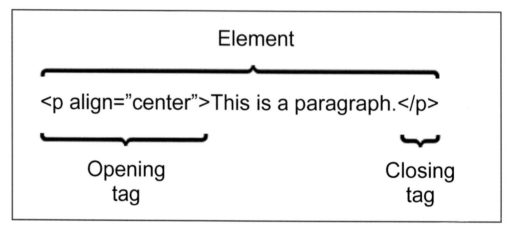

- The text in the paragraph is contained by two **tags:** an opening <p> tag and a closing </p> tag.
- The **element** is made up of the opening <p> and closing </p> *including the text between them*.
- The **attribute** sits inside the opening tag. In this case, it is an alignment attribute.

So just to be clear, a tag is a pair of angled brackets with letters written between these brackets e.g. <p>. Tags come in pairs: an opening tag and a closing tag. The closing tag differs from the opening tag because it has a forward slash character after the left angled bracket. Elements are opening and closing tags plus whatever is between them. Attributes are additional instructions contained within the opening tag in an element.

The attribute in our example indicates that the text in the paragraph should be aligned to the centre of the document, just like centring text in a word processor. (Note that the American English spelling of center is used in HTML.)

Attributes tend to follow a simple structure. They have:

- **An attribute name**. This is the property of the element that the attribute applies to, such as the alignment of text.
- **An attribute value**. This is the setting for this property, which for the align attribute can be left, right, center or justify.

There is always an equals sign separating the attribute name from its value and the value should be written within double quotes (although not all web page authors do this).

You will often see elements and attributes written in upper case, lower case, or indeed a mix of both. However, in XHTML (which we think of as being the most recent version of HTML), all element and attribute names should be written in lower case.

The skeleton of a web page

There are a few elements which you should always include whenever you create a web page. When we saw the first very basic example of a web page on p.125, we just looked at about half of the lines (the headings and the paragraphs). Let's go back to that example now, this time taking a look at the elements in the code.

Here is the code for that document again. The bits highlighted in grey are the parts that should appear in each document. We have indented elements that are inside other elements because it makes them easier to read.

```
<html>
 <head><title>My First Web Page</title></head>
 <body>

  <h1>Main Heading for the Page</h1>
  <p>First paragraph contains some text
     describing that this is my first web page.
     Even if this page seems very simple, soon I
     will be creating much more complex pages.</p>

  <h2>Here is a subheading</h2>
  <p>Here is a second paragraph under a
     subheading</p>

 </body>
</html>
```

So ... every HTML page should start with an opening <html> tag and end with a closing </html> tag. The page is contained within these two tags and is divided into two sections:

● The **head** of the document, contained between an opening <head> and a closing </head> tag. The head of the document contains information about the document but it is not actually visible when the page is viewed in a browser.
● The **body** of a document, contained between an opening <body> and closing </body> element. This is what you see in the browser window. In other words, it's the real content of the page.

Inside the <head> element there should be a <title> element. This is the page title and is usually displayed in the very top line of the browser window, outside the page content.

The <title> element is shown above the main browser menu.

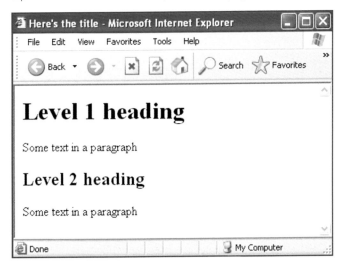

PART **Creating your first web page**

Now that we know the basic structure of a web page, let's try building one from scratch.

1

Open up a text editor such as Windows Notepad (click Start > Programs > Accessories > Notepad) or SimpleText or TextEdit on a Mac.

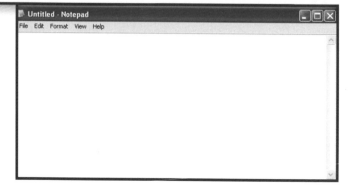

2

Enter the opening <html> tag at the top of the document, and a closing </html> tag at the bottom, leaving a couple of blank lines in between.

3

Add the opening and closing <head></head> tags followed by the <body></body> tags. Indenting tags as shown here can help you keep track of your code.

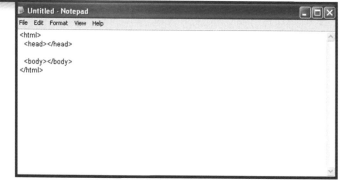

Inside the <head> element add the <title> element, with the words "My First Web Page" inside that. This completes the skeleton of the web page.

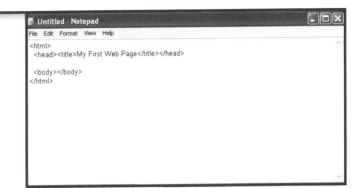

Now we'll look at the main part of the page. Inside the <body> element add a <h1> element containing the words "My Home Page". Again, indent the element to make the code clear.

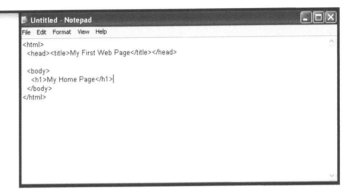

Add a <p> element after the <h1> element to create a paragraph. This paragraph should contain the words "Welcome to my first web page".

Save the file on your desktop as example1.html. If your text editor decides to save it as example.html.txt instead – that is, with a .txt extension at the end of the file name – put the name of the file in double quotes. This time it should save as a web page. Now start up your favourite web browser and go to the File menu. Select Open and browse to the file you just saved. You should see something like this: a bona fide web page created with nothing but HTML code in a text editor. Congratulations!

PART 5 Taking it further

Having seen the basic structure of a web page and learned the difference between elements (which are made up of tags and what is between those tags) and attributes, you can quickly look at a whole range of other elements, and start creating far more complicated and interesting documents.

But before we press on, note that you can learn a lot about web page structure simply by looking at how other people go about writing their web pages. This is because browsers have an option which reveals the source code behind a page. In Internet Explorer go to the View menu, and select the View Source option. Here we can see the source code for the website homepage of the W3C (the body that controls the development of HTML).

Viewing the source of pages is a great way to learn more.

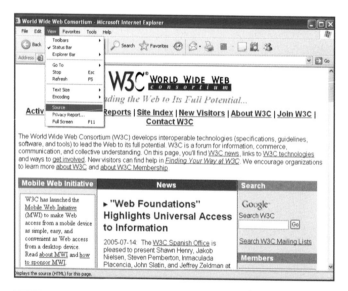

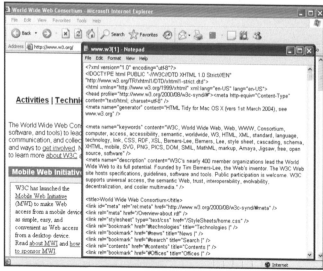

If you have already had a look at the source of some web pages, you might have seen the <body> element carry all kinds of attributes, such as bgcolor (which can be used to set the background colour of the document) or leftmargin (which is just one way to offset the page from the edge of the browser window). But remember that we are not using attributes to change the appearance of our documents. Rather, as we shall see, that is a job for CSS.

You might also see elements called <script>, which usually contain a language called JavaScript. Unfortunately, there is not space to go into scripting in this book.

Using elements to markup text

In this section, we will take a closer look at several elements that can be used to describe the structure of a web page. Keep focussing on that word *structure* as you read through this section: we are trying to describe the overall layout of the documents, not its appearance.

<h1> to <h6> contain headings

In the same way that your word processor has several "levels" of heading, starting with heading 1 for the primary heading, heading 2 for section headings, heading 3 for sub-headings within sections and so on, there are six levels of heading in HTML. These are represented using the elements <h1> to <h6>.

By default, a browser will display <h1> elements in the largest size and <h6> elements in the smallest, as you can see here:

How a browser renders heading elements.

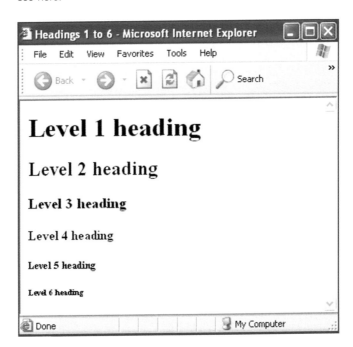

<p> contains paragraphs

As we have already seen, each heading is likely to be followed by one or more paragraphs of text. The opening <p> tag indicates the start of a paragraph, while the end of a paragraph is shown with a closing </p> tag.

 creates a line break

The <br /> element creates a line break (a bit like pressing the return key when using a word processor). The <br /> element is a special kind of element because it does not need a closing tag. It is referred to as an "empty element". Empty elements need to be written with a space and a forward slash character before the right angled bracket.

You could write sentences on consecutive lines like so:

Line one
Line two
Line three
Line four
Line five

Sometimes you might see a line break simply written <br>, but it is good practice to write them correctly, like this: <br />.

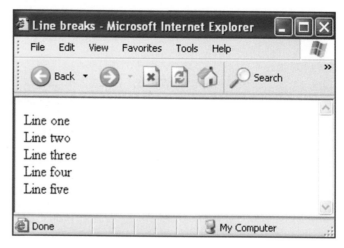

Creating line breaks with the <br /> element.

<pre> creates preformatted text

One interesting thing about web browsers is that they will only show one space between two words, even if you type 20 spaces in your web page. However, if you want the spaces to be preserved in part of a page, then you can write that content in a <pre> element.

The real purpose of a <pre> element is to preserve the precise formatting of the text when this is important to its understanding, such as when writing computer code. It should not be used simply to add line breaks (for which you should use the <br /> element), or to indent text (for which you should use CSS).

As this screenshot shows, browsers tend to format the contents of a <pre> element in a type of font referred to as "monospace". In a monospace font, each letter is the same width whereas, in other fonts, letters like "m" are wider than letters like "l".

You can retain spaces and line breaks using a <pre> element.

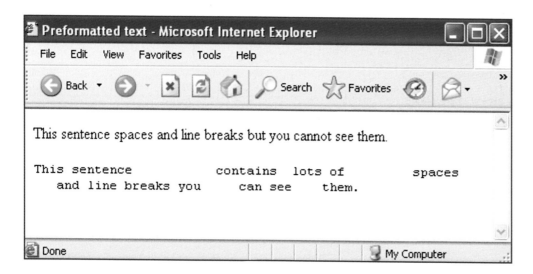

Presentational elements

Now let's take a look at some elements that affect the presentation of text. These are fairly self-explanatory, so they are just listed in the following table.

Element	Purpose
<b>	Bold. The content of the element will be displayed in a bold typeface.
<i>	Italic. The content of the element will be displayed in an italic typeface.
<u>	Underline. The content of the element will be underlined.
<strike>	Strikethrough. The content of the element will have a line through the centre of the font.
<sup>	Superscript. The content of the element will be shown in superscript (a smaller font that looks higher than the rest of the text on that line). It is commonly used with dates, as in 12th.
<sub>	Subscript. The content of the element will be shown in subscript (a smaller font which looks lower that the rest of the text on that line). It is commonly used to denote footnotes.
<small>	The content of the element will be shown smaller than the surrounding text.
<big>	The content of the element will be shown bigger than the surrounding text.
<hr />	An empty element that creates a horizontal line, also known as a horizontal rule.

Here is an example that makes use of some of the presentational elements:

```
<html>
  <head><title>Presentational
  Elements</title></head>
  <body>
    <b>Here is some bold text</b><br />
    <i>Here is some italic text</i><br />
    <u>This text is underlined</u><br />
    <strike>This text has a line through
    it</strike><br />
    You can add superscript text, for things
    such as dates: 12<sup>th</sup> July<br />
    You can add subscript for things like
    footnotes <sub>2</sub><br />
    You can make some text <small>smaller than
    the text</small> surrounding it<br />
    You can make some text <big>bigger than the
    text</big> surrounding it<br />
    <hr />
  </body>
</html>
```

You can see what this page looks like here:

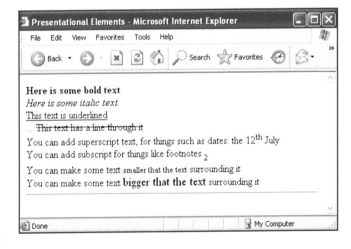

Presentational elements affect the look of their contents.

Phrase elements

Phrase elements add to the meaning of the document. Some of these elements will be displayed slightly differently in a web browser, although they should never be used for the way they make text look. Again, appearance is the role of CSS.

In fact, a couple of these elements are not for the benefit of those looking at websites, but rather for other types of program.

Element	Purpose
<em>	Emphasis. This indicates that the content of this element should have emphasis. Voice browsers (used by the blind) would add emphasis when reading the content of this element. Most browsers show emphasis in italic text.
<strong>	Strong emphasis. As with the <em> element, this adds emphasis, but this time it is strong emphasis. Most browsers show this in bold text.
<address>	Address. You should place addresses inside an address element to help automated applications (such as search engines) isolate addresses in web pages.
<code>	Computer code. This will tend to be preformatted and shown in a fixed-width font such as courier.

Here is an example that uses phrase elements:

```
<html>
    <head><title>Phrase Elements</title></head>
    <body>
        You can add <em>emphasis</em><br />
        You can add <strong>strong
        emphasis</strong><br /><br />
        The Queen of England's main residence is
        <address>Buckingham Palace, Buckingham
        Palace Road, London, SW1A 1AA,
        UK</address><br /><br />
        Code has a special element
        <code>print()</code>
    </body>
</html>
```

You can see what this example looks like in a browser in this screenshot:

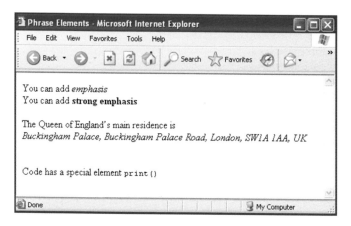

Phrase elements add meaning to their content.

Lists

If you want to add a list to your web page, with either bullet points or numbers, then there are some special elements that allow you to do this.

Element	Purpose
<ul>	Unordered list, denoted with bullet points
<ol>	Ordered list, numbered
<li>	List item, delimiting each separate entry in the list

Here we have an example of ordered and unordered lists:

```
<html>
   <head><title>Example of lists</title></head>
   <body>

   Here is an example of a bulleted list:
   <ul>
      <li>Bullet point one</li>
      <li>Bullet point two</li>
      <li>Bullet point three</li>
   </ul>

   Here is an example of a numbered list:
   <ol>
      <li>Item number one</li>
      <li>Item number two</li>
      <li>Item number three</li>
   </ol>

   </body>
</html>
```

There are also a couple of handy attributes that you might like to be aware of when creating numbered lists. The type attribute sits in the opening <ol> tag and allows you to specify what numbers you want to use. For example:

Attribute	Purpose
<ol type="1">	Creates numbers (1, 2, 3)
<ol type="A">	Creates upper case letters (A, B, C)
<ol type="a">	Creates lower case letters (a, b, c)
<ol type="I">	Creates upper case Roman numerals (I, II, III
<ol type="i">	Creates lower case Roman numerals (i, ii, iii)

You can also indicate what number you want your list to start at by using the start attribute. This sits in the opening <ol> tag in an ordered list. For example, the following list would start with the number 3:

```
<ol start="3">
   <li>list item 3</li>
   <li>list item 4</li>
   <li>list item 5</li>
</ol>
```

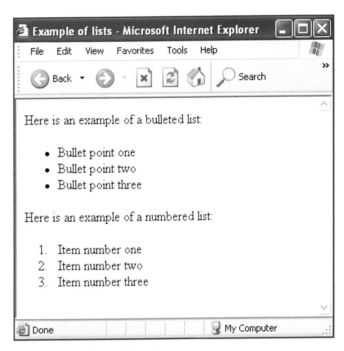

You can create bullet points and numbered lists.

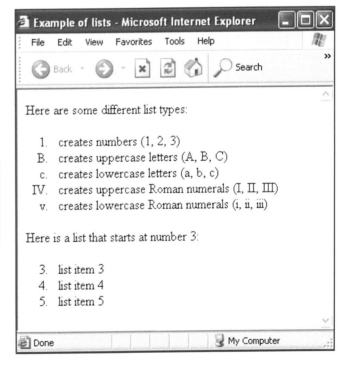

You can select the type of numbered list and the starting number.

137

The <font> element

As we mentioned earlier in the chapter, some elements were introduced into HTML just to grant web page authors the ability to control the presentation of their pages. One such element was the <font> element which allows you to specify what kind of typeface you want to use in your document (for example, to specify that text should be shown in Arial, Courier or some other typeface). While it is now generally considered better to use CSS rather than HTML to control the presentation of your pages, you will still often see the <font> element used.

The <font> element can carry several useful attributes, such as:

- **Face**. This value is a comma-separated list of typefaces, starting with your first choice and then stating alternatives. A browser can only display any given typeface if that font is installed on the computer, so it pays to give alternatives and to stick to commonly used fonts rather than going for something exotic.
- **Size**. This value determines the size of the typeface, ranging from 1 (smallest) to 6 (largest).
- **Color**. This value controls the typeface colour. Note the American spelling.

For example, you might see a page that uses the <font> element like so:

```
<html>
   <head><title>A page that uses the font
   element</title></head>
   <body>
      <font face="arial, verdana, sans-serif"
      size="6" color="red">Heading goes
      here</font><br>
      <font face="times, times new roman, serif"
      size="2" color="black">The text underneath
      the heading goes here.</font>
   </body>
</html>
```

You can see what this page would look like here:

The <font> element is still widely used, but you should try to use CSS, rather than markup, to control the presentation of pages.

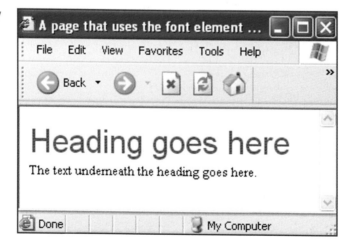

PART 5

Creating links between pages

One of the most powerful features of the web has long been and remains hyperlinks (or just links, for short), by which we mean text or images that you can click on to move to another page. Although we take links for granted, without the ability to link between documents the web would not have been anywhere near as popular as it is today.

In this section we will be looking at how to create four types of links:

● Links from your page to another website
● Links to other pages on your own site
● Links to a specific part of a page
● Email links

Creating links to other websites

If you want to add a link to another website, you can do this with the <a>, the anchor, element. When people click on the text between the opening <a> tag and the closing </a> tag they get transported to another page.

The address of the page you want to link to is specified using the href attribute. For example, the following would create a link to the Google website:

```
<a href="http://www.google.com">Google is a
popular search engine</a>
```

The text between the <a> tags becomes a clickable link.

As we can see from the screenshot, by default the text between the opening <a> tag and the closing </a> tag is usually shown in blue in the browser, and will be underlined. We will learn later how to change the presentation of links using CSS.

You can change the behaviour of a hyperlink so that clicking it opens the new web page in a new browser window (rather than replacing the current page with the new page). To do this, use the target attribute and give it a value of _blank, like so:

```
<a href="http://www.google.com"
target="_blank">Google is a popular search
engine</a>
```

This link will look exactly the same as the previous one when viewed on the page, but it will open in a new browser window. You should avoid opening too many pages in new windows as web users can get very confused if there are lots of windows open at the same time. As a result, most web page authors avoid opening new windows for web pages on their own site, and only create a new window if they are linking to another site altogether.

Creating links to pages on your own site

Creating links to pages on your own site can be even easier than creating links to other sites. If you have several web pages that are all in the same folder, you only need to put the name of the file in the value of the href attribute on the opening <a> tag. For example, here is a link to a page called ContactUs.html that lives in the same folder as this page:

```
<a href="ContactUs.html">Contact details</a>
```

However, if you have a large site with lots of pages, you are likely to want to arrange these pages into separate folders in order to help you keep track of each of the pages. For example, a music website might have the following sections: home page, news, reviews, events, contact us.

If the site owners regularly update its content, they might put the news, reviews and events each in their own separate folders to help keep track of the pages. The folder structure might look something like the one shown in this screenshot:

Large sites can separate their page sections, each with their own folder.

The home page in this case is called index.html. The home page is not in a folder, so in order to link to a news page called news.html in the news folder, the link should specify the name of the folder followed by a forward slash followed by the name of the file in that folder:

```
<a href="news/news.html">News Home Page</a>
```

And if this same news page wanted to link back to the main home page called index.html then that link would start with two dots and a forward slash, to indicate that the file was in the parent folder:

```
<a href="../index.html">News Home Page</a>
```

These partial addresses (which do not start with a domain name, such as **http://www.haynes.co.uk**) are known as **relative addresses** because they point to pages in **relation** to the position of this page. There are two great advantages to using relative URLs on your own site:

● They are much shorter and are therefore quicker to write.
● If your domain name changes (which can happen if you get a new hosting company) you do not have to rewrite all of your links. They will continue to work so long as you preserve your folder structure.

Creating links to parts of pages

You have probably seen some web pages that contain links to specific parts of the same page. For example, a long page might have a list of links at the top of the page to help you find the appropriate part of the page (FAQ pages are a good example of this).

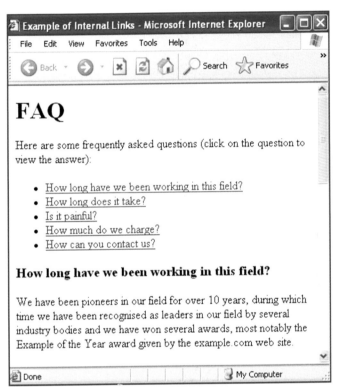

On a long page, you might want to create a link to a specific part of the page.

In such cases there are two parts to the links:

- **Source**: the link the user clicks on to get taken to another part of a page.
- **Destination**: the part of the page they will arrive at.

Both are created with the <a> element, but they carry different attributes. Let's have a look at the destination link first, because without that we don't have a specific part of the page to link to.

The destination part of the link is an <a> element in the part of the document you want to link to. When the <a> element is a destination, it should have two attributes: name and id. The value of these attributes should be the same and it should be a name/word to identify that part of the page. For example, on long pages you might create a destination at the top of your page, and create a link from the bottom of the page back up to the top. In this case, let's say you want to return a visitor to your first heading, like so:

```
<a name="top" id="top"><h1>My Home Page</h1></a>
```

The words "My Home Page" are thus marked up as a destination. With the destination in place, you can now add the source part of the link further down the page so that when people click the link, the browser window will scroll back up to "My Home Page" (the destination).

When source links are pointing to a part of the same page, they have an href attribute whose value starts with a # sign, like so:

```
<a href="#top">Back to top</a>
```

The viewer will now see the phrase "Back to top" as an underlined blue hyperlink on the page; and when they click it, they'll be whisked back to the top of the page.

You can also link to a specific part of *another* page in your website. For example, if you had a long FAQ page, you might want to link *to* a specific question on that part of the page *from* several places on the site. The question is thus the destination.

If one of the items in your FAQ was your contact details, the relevant part of the FAQ page (which is called faq.html) might look like this:

```
<a name="contact" id="contact"><h2>How to contact
us</h2></a>
<p>You can call us on 0800 000 000 or email
help@example.com</p>
```

This is the destination, marked up with a name and id attributes. You could then link to this part of the faq.html page using a source link like this:

```
<a href="faq.html#contact">How to contact us</a>
```

Note the syntax. The file name (i.e. the name of the web page we want to link to) is followed by the # symbol followed by the value of the name or id attribute on the destination.

Creating links to send emails

You can even create special links that launch the visitor's default email program. To create an email link you need to use the <a> element again. Users can click on whatever is written between the opening <a> tag and the closing </a> tag in order to send the email.

This time, the value of the href attribute starts with the keyword mailto, followed by a colon, followed by the email address you are sending the message to:

```
<a href="mailto:info@example.com">Send me an email</a>
```

All you would see in the browser is a link that says send me an email. When the user clicks it, their email program will open a new, blank email addressed to the specified email address.

You can even create links that add a pre-determined subject line to the email. In order to do this, add a question mark after the email address, followed by the subject of the message. Note that if your subject line contains spaces, as it will if it's more than one word, you must replace the spaces with the characters %20, like so:

```
<a href="mailto:info@example.com?subject=website%20enquiry">Send me an email</a>
```

You can use email links to encourage users to send you emails.

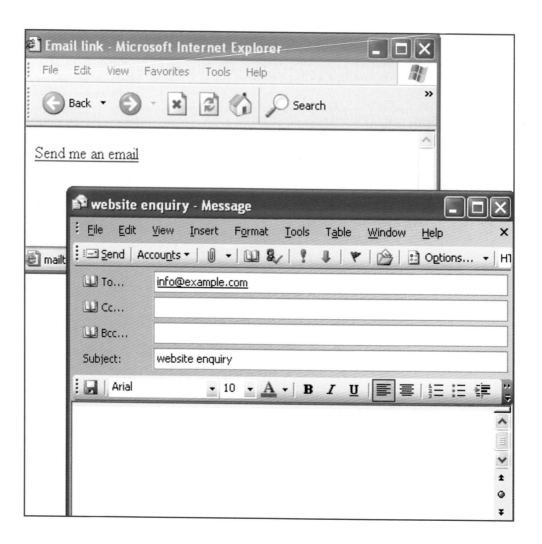

142

PART 5

Adding images to your pages

Images really help liven up any website. If pages are too text heavy, they can put visitors off. Photos, logos and images for the main navigation all have a place and images can be made into clickable links in much the same way as text.

However, you should be careful about your use of images. If you use too many, or if they are too large, the page will be slow to load. This is less of a problem if your visitors are coming to your site over a broadband internet connection but this should not be taken for granted.

The <img /> element

You can insert images into your pages using the <img /> element. It is another example of an empty element (like the <br /> and <hr /> elements) and therefore only one tag is used. This tag should carry several attributes, and it should end with a space and a forward slash before the right angled bracket.

Images should generally be stored along with the pages of your site, and they are often put in a special folder called **images** (or sometimes called assets). Here we can see a folder structure for the music site we discussed on p.140, this time with an added images folder.

Images are often placed in a folder of their own. In this case, you can see an images folder.

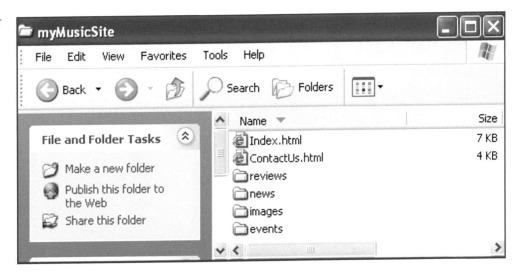

The name of the image that you want to use is given as the value of an attribute called src. For example, if you want to add a logo (logo.gif) to the home page of the music site (index.html), and that image was in the images folder, you could do it like so:

```
<img src="images/logo.gif" />
```

You can see that the image is identified in the same way as the relative URLs we met on pp.140–1. If you wanted to add this same image to a page in the news folder called news.html, then you would write it like so:

```
<img src="../images/logo.gif" />
```

In this case, the ../ indicates that we need to go up a folder and then look in the images folder.

<img /> elements should also always carry an alt attribute. The value of the alt attribute is a text description for the image, so this element might look like this:

```
<img src="../images/logo.gif" alt="MyMusicSite
Logo" />
```

Ideally, you should also control the width and the height of the image here, measured in pixels. These measurements are given in width and height attributes, like so:

```
<img src="../images/logo.gif" alt="MyMusicSite
Logo" width="150" height="40" />
```

This shows an image that is 150 pixels wide and 40 pixels high. To find the size of an existing image, simply open it in your web browser, right-click it and select Properties. Here you will see an option that says Dimensions.

Right-clicking an image in a browser and selecting the Properties option shows you the image dimensions. You can change these with the width and height attributes.

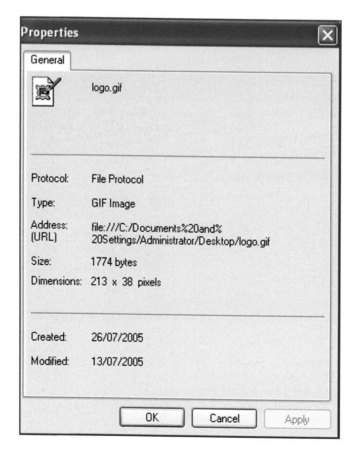

What types of image to use

There are lots of image formats that you can choose from, but it is best to stick to two types of image for the web: GIF and JPEG. As a rule of thumb, use GIF images for graphics that contain a lot of flat colour (for example, a logo with areas that have the same shade of red) and JPEGs for photographs. This is because GIF images will save to smaller file sizes when parts of the photo use exactly the same colours, and JPEGs are better for saving images where there are lots of different colours.

Many browsers also support a format called PNG, which was designed to be the successor to the GIF image. Unfortunately, image formats other than GIF and JPEG work in some browsers but not in others, and so are best avoided. Any good image manipulation program (such as Photoshop or Paint Shop Pro) will allow you to save images as GIFs or JPEGs.

It is worth noting that the maximum computer screen resolution is 72 dots per inch (72dpi), which is a lot lower than print resolution. Images with a higher resolution than 72dpi will take longer to load than necessary and will not look any better on screen. Use your image editor to reduce the resolution to 72dpi before using images on the web.

If your image is a photo you should use a JPEG.

If an image contains sections that are exactly the same colour, you should save it as a GIF. This is typically used for computer-generated graphics.

Using images as links

You can put an image between an opening <a> tag and a closing </a> tag to make an image a link. If you do, you should also add a border attribute with a value of 0 otherwise you will find a blue line drawn around the edge of your image. For example:

```
<a href="index.html"><img
src="../images/logo.gif" alt="MyMusicSite Logo"
border="0" /></a>
```

This screenshot shows you an example of two images, the first without a border attribute, and the second with a border attribute whose value is 0.

If you make an image a link, you will have to add a border attribute to prevent an unsightly blue line appearing around the edge of it.

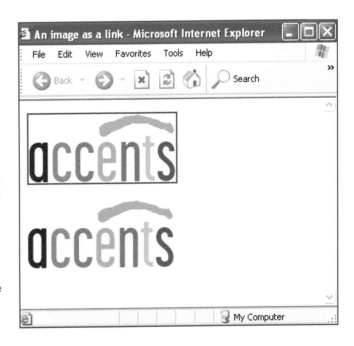

Where to get images

It can be very hard to find strong images that really set off your site. However, it is well worth spending the time on getting the right images as it can make the difference between an average site and a great site.

Generally speaking you cannot just copy images from other people's sites. This would be breaking copyright law. Many professional web designers either pay for the right to use photos from what is known as a stock photography library (such as **www.gettyimages.com** or **www.corbis.com**) or sometimes even commission original photographs.

However, there are some good resources on the web where you can find very cheap images. iStockPhoto, **www.iStockPhoto.com**, was set up for web designers to get cheap stock photography and for photographers and illustrators to sell their pictures. Prices start at US$1 per photo (compared to the £50+ per photo charged by many image libraries). See also p.43.

www.iStockPhoto.com is a great resource for finding good quality, reasonably priced images for your sites.

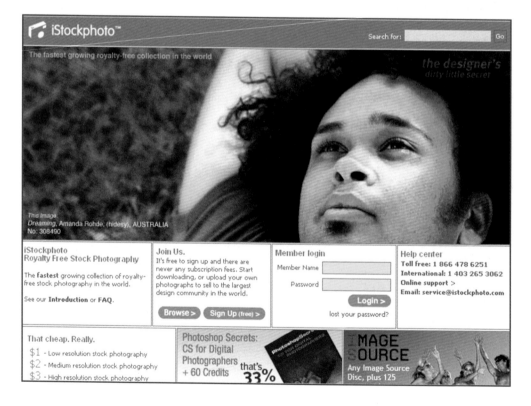

PART 5

Adding tables to your pages

The ability to create tables is a very handy part of a web designer's toolkit. There are two main reasons why you might want to add tables to your site:

● You have some tabular data, which is best organised in rows and columns, such as sporting results or research findings.
● You want to control the layout of your pages, in which case tables can be used to position items on your page.

We're going to take a look at creating tables for tabular data first.

Tables for tabular data

Tables are created using an element called – no surprises here – <table>. The table is held between the opening <table> tag and a closing </table> tag. Between these tags, tables are written out one row at a time, using the <tr> element to create a table row. Each row is then made up of individual table cells, from left to right. These cells are created using one of two elements:

● The <th> element indicates a table heading
● The <td> element indicates a table data cell

As with the other elements we met earlier, the content must go between the opening and closing tags. Take a look at this simple table:

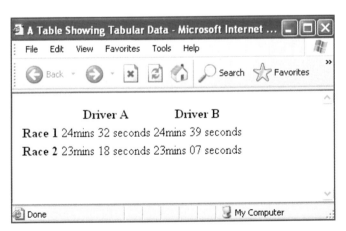

A table with three rows and three columns.

Here is the code used to create this page. Note how the markup for the tables is indented, as this makes it easier to read:

```
<table>
    <tr>
        <td></td>
        <th>Driver A</th>
        <th>Driver B</th>
    </tr>
    <tr>
        <th>Race 1</th>
        <td>24 mins 32 seconds</td>
        <td>24 mins 39 seconds </td>
    </tr>
    <tr>
        <th>Race 2</th>
        <td>23 mins 18 seconds </td>
        <td>23 mins 07 seconds </td>
    </tr>
</table>
```

As you can see the entire table is contained within a <table> element. The three rows each start with an opening <tr> tag and end with a closing </tr> tag. Inside each row are three more elements. Some of these are headings, others are table data.

Each row should have the same number of cells, even if some of those cells are empty (whether they are <th> or <td> elements).

Table borders and spacing

The table element can carry a border attribute to determine the width of the border in pixels. For example, to create a table with no border you would have the following:

```
<table border="0">
```

To have a 10 pixel wide border you would have the following:

```
<table border="10">
```

You can add space between each of the cells using the cellspacing attribute. The value of this attribute is the gap between cells in pixels:

```
<table border="2" cellspacing="10">
```

You can add space between the edge of the cell and what is written inside it using the cellpadding attribute:

```
<table border="2" cellpadding="10">
```

Here you can see some examples of different borders, cellpaddings, and cellspacings:

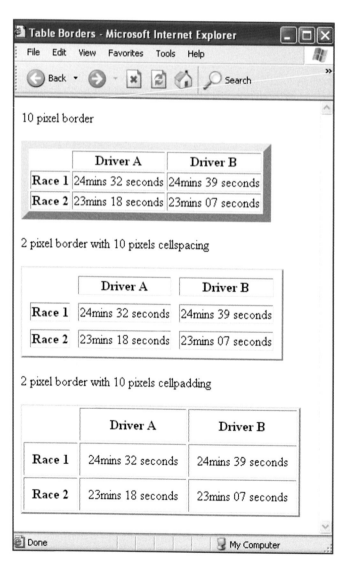

You can easily control the appearance of your tables.

Table and cell widths

You can control the width of the entire table with the width attribute on the <table> element, and you can control the width of columns by using the width attribute on the first set of <td> or <th> elements in the table (note that you cannot have different widths for cells in different rows).

```
<table width="500" border="1">
   <tr>
      <td width="250"></td>
      <th width="125">Driver A</th>
      <th width="125">Driver B</th>
   </tr>
   <tr>
      <th>Race 1</th>
      <td>24 mins 32 seconds</td>
      <td>24 mins 39 seconds </td>
   </tr>
   <tr>
      <th>Race 2</th>
      <td>23 mins 18 seconds </td>
      <td>23 mins 07 seconds </td>
   </tr>
</table>
```

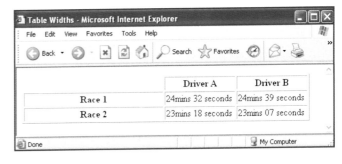

Controlling the width of tables and cells.

Using tables for layout

As you can see, tables create a grid. Often when print designers are creating a page layout they will use a **layout grid**, which divides pages into columns and rows. For example, traditional newspapers often display articles in columns. Web designers do something very similar by using tables to layout web pages. It helps them to create columns of text and images that sit next to each other.

Here you can see an example of a site designed with borderless (and thus invisible) tables:

Research has showed that people have difficulty reading large amounts of text on the web, especially when they are shown in wide lines, so restricting the width of text makes it easier on the eye. It can also make the page look more attractive. Here is the same page designed without a table in place to control the positioning of the text.

Using a table is also one way of ensuring that your page remains a fixed width; no matter what the size of the viewer's browser window, you can control the way your page content is displayed by placing it within a fixed-width table.

You can control the layout of your pages with tables.

Same page as before – but this time without using tables.

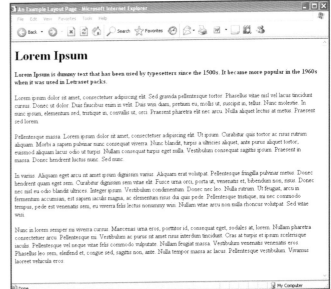

Vertical alignment of text

If the cells on a row contain different amounts of text, vertical text positioning defaults to the middle of the cell. You can make text align from the top of the cell, which generally looks better, using the valign attribute (this attribute can also take values of middle and bottom).

Using the valign attribute to control the vertical alignment of table cells.

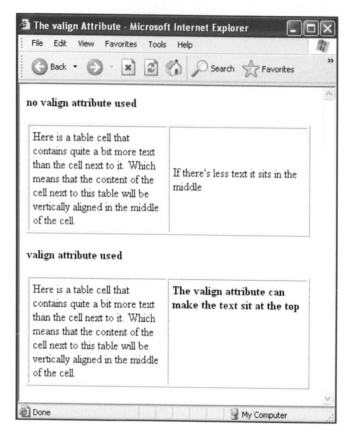

Nesting elements

As we have seen, most elements, with the exception of empty elements such as <br /> and <hr />, have starting and ending tags. It is very important to write these tags symmetrically – or to give it the correct term, to make sure that they nest correctly.

If you place an element within another element, both the opening and closing tags must appear within that element. So if you want some bold text in a paragraph, for example, your opening and closing <b> tags both need to be inside the <p> element.

An example would probably help here. The following is correct, because both the opening and closing tag of the <b> element are inside the <p> element:

```
<p>At the end of this paragraph is some <b>bold
text</b></p>
```

However, the following is incorrect, because the closing <b> tag is outside the closing <p> tag:

```
<p>At the end of this paragraph is some <b>bold
text</p></b>
```

While most browsers would still display this example as you would hope, it is technically incorrect, and it is a good idea to get into the habit of closing all elements correctly.

PART

Creating your first site – using HTML

In this workshop, we are going to put together what we have learned so far and create a very simple two-page site. The first page will introduce the subject – you – and the second page will talk about your hobbies and interests:

1

Open up your text editor (such as Windows Notepad or TextEdit). We will start by creating a home page that introduces you.

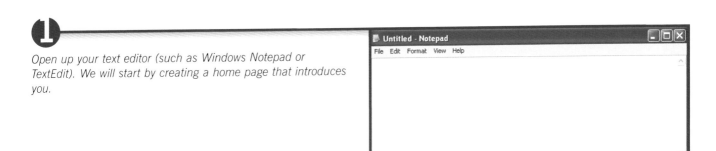

2

Add the skeleton of the page, the <html>, <head>, <title> and <body> elements. The title of the page will be your name followed by the words "Home Page".

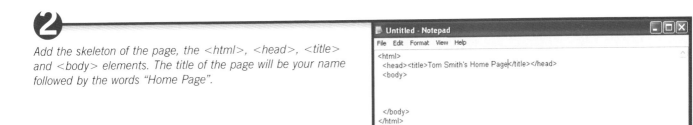

3

In the body of the page, we will put an <h1> element to contain the title of the page. This will be followed by a <p> element containing the name of this page and a link to the second page of the site. The content of this paragraph is what allows users to understand the structure of the site and navigate it. You can see from a glance that there is a Home page (this page) and a page about your hobbies. To get the hobby page, simply click on this link. You could easily add more pages to the site by adding more links to this section when you have created the page.

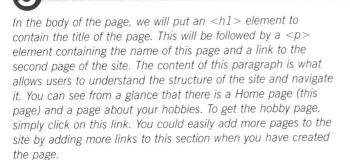

4

Next add in an introductory paragraph introducing yourself, your name and age, where you live, and where you work.

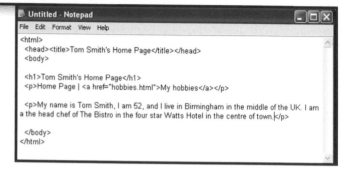

5

Add a paragraph about your family. Inside this paragraph, add an <img /> element linking to a picture of yourself. Make sure that the photo is stored in the same folder on your computer as this page. Speaking of which…

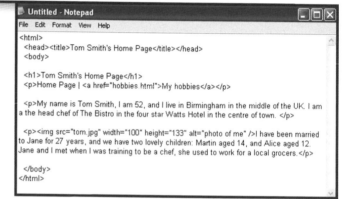

6

Save this page as index.html. As just mentioned, this file and the photo should be saved in the same folder.

Now open a second blank page in your text editor and add in the skeleton of the HTML document. This time the title of the page should be your name followed by the word "Hobbies".

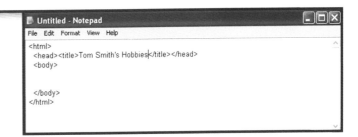

Again, add a level 1 heading, followed by a paragraph containing the names of the pages in the site. This time, the "Home Page" text should have an <a> element to make a link to the home page.

Add an unordered list, with at least three points. Each of these points should contain the name of one of your hobbies.

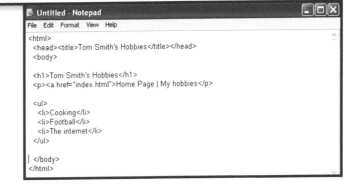

For each of these points, add a level 2 heading, followed by a paragraph about that hobby.

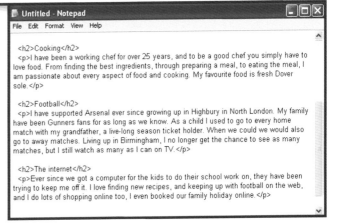

Around each <h2> element add a destination anchor, so that
you can link directly to this part of the page.

```
    <a name="cooking" id="cooking"><h2>Cooking</h2></a>
    <p>I have been a working chef for over 25 years, and to be a good chef you simply have to
love food. From finding the best ingredients, through preparing a meal, to eating the meal, I
am passionate about every aspect of food and cooking. My favourite food is fresh Dover
sole.</p>

    <a name="football" id="football"><h2>Football</h2></a>
    <p>I have supported Arsenal ever since growing up in Highbury in North London. My family
have been Gunners fans for as long as we know. As a child I used to go to every home
match with my grandfather, a live-long season ticket holder. When we could we would also
go to away matches. Living up in Birmingham, I no longer get the chance to see as many
matches, but I still watch as many as I can on TV.</p>

    <a name="internet" id="internet"><h2>The internet</h2></a>
    <p>Ever since we got a computer for the kids to do their school work on, they have been
trying to keep me off it. I love finding new recipes, and keeping up with football on the web,
and I do lots of shopping online too, I even booked our family holiday online.</p>
```

In the <li> elements at the top of the page, add links to these
destination anchors, so people can skip directly to each part of
the page.

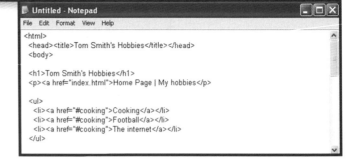

```
<html>
  <head><title>Tom Smith's Hobbies</title></head>
  <body>

  <h1>Tom Smith's Hobbies</h1>
  <p><a href="index.html">Home Page | My hobbies</p>

  <ul>
    <li><a href="#cooking">Cooking</a></li>
    <li><a href="#cooking">Football</a></li>
    <li><a href="#cooking">The internet</a></li>
  </ul>
```

Save the file as hobbies.html.

Open up index.html in your browser, and you can now see and browse your first small site. OK, it's not actually on the internet but traditional sites are usually designed and built offline like this (unlike blogs, which are created and developed live online). We'll return to this point later.

6

PART **6**

BUILD YOUR OWN WEBSITE

Adding style to your documents

PART **Style sheets**

We've looked at how to markup text and create document structures, and how to create links and add images to web pages. It's about time we thought about making pages more attractive.

In order to control the presentation of the pages we need to work with a language that is used in conjunction with HTML. This is called CSS or Cascading Style Sheets.

A cascading style sheet is made up of rules that are applied to the content of certain elements in order to indicate how these elements should be formatted. For example, you might set rules that control the typeface used for the content of the <h1> element, making all level one headings a different style from the rest of the text on the page. Similarly, you might want to set the background colour of table heading elements so that they stand out from the rest of the table.

These rules can be placed inside the <head> element of a document using an element called <style>. However, you are generally better off creating a separate CSS file which can then be linked to and referenced by all your HTML pages. This is the approach we will be taking. All we need, again, is a text editor like Notepad.

How to link to a style sheet
You can use the same CSS style sheet with all the pages on your site. This can save a great deal of work because you do not have to put markup in each separate page to indicate how the page should look. To link to a CSS file from your HTML documents, you need to put a <link /> element inside the <head> element on each page. The <link /> element is an empty element:

```
<link rel="stylesheet" type="text/css"
href="styles.css" />
```

The <link /> element is not only used with style sheets, so it carries three attributes that describe the document being linked to:

- The rel attribute (short for relationship). This indicates the relationship between the current document and the one in the link. In this case, it indicates that the document being linked to is a style sheet for this document.
- The type attribute. This indicates the media type of document that is being linked to. In this case the file is a style sheet, which is a text document (as opposed to a JPEG, an MP3 or some other kind of file).
- The href attribute. This determines where the style sheet can be found. Here the style sheet is called "styles.css" and is in the same folder as the page.

Advantages of using external style sheets
Here are just a few of the advantages you achieve by using external style sheets to control the presentation of your web pages rather than using markup in your HTML documents that controls presentation of pages:

- You can use the same style sheet with several HTML pages rather than repeating the rules in each page.
- You can easily update the look of a whole site simply by updating the rules in the style sheet (rather than altering each page individually).
- A style sheet can act as a template to help different web page authors achieve the same style settings.
- A style sheet makes your pages more accessible to those with visual impairments.

Associating rules with elements

As we mentioned, a style sheet is made up of rules. Each rule applies to certain elements (and usually any elements within that element too). There are two parts to any rule:

The selector indicates which elements the rule applies to. These are written without the angled brackets, so p indicates that a rule should apply to the <p> element.

The declaration indicates how the elements in the selector should be styled.

A style sheet rule consists of a selector and a declaration.

The declaration lives inside curly braces and is also split into two parts separated by a colon:

● The property determines which aspect of the element you want to affect (e.g. the colour or typeface used).
● The value specifies the setting for the property (e.g. the colour red or the typeface Arial).

A declaration can be made up of multiple property/value pairs, so you can control several aspects of an element in a single rule. Multiple declarations should be separated by semi-colons (and can be written on the same or different lines). Let's look at a simple example of a CSS rule:

```
p {
   font-family:Arial, Verdana, sans-serif;
   font-weight:bold;
   font-size:12px;}
```

This rule applies to <p> elements, and indicates that the text inside <p> elements should be displayed in an Arial typeface (and if the user doesn't have Arial, then the text should be shown in Verdana, and if they do not have Verdana installed, then the computer's default sans-serif font). It also indicates that the paragraph should be a bold typeface whose size is 12 pixels.

You can also indicate that the declarations apply to more than one element by separating multiple element names with commas. So, if the selector for this example was p, td then these declarations would apply to both <p> and <td> elements.

So, a style sheet is a file that contains one or more of these rules, which govern the overall appearance of web pages. It can be written in a text editor, such as Windows Notepad or TextEdit on a Mac, and should be saved with a .css file extension.

Class and id selectors

CSS allows for some much more complex selectors. There are whole (dull) books dedicated to CSS and we don't have space to go into every aspect of the language here, but there are two special kinds of selector that we should mention:

- Class selectors
- id selectors

Every element that appears in the body of an HTML page can carry an attribute called class and an attribute called id:

- id attributes are used to uniquely identify an element within a document (no two elements in the same document should share the same value for the id attribute).
- Class attributes are used to identify groups of elements. For example, you might want to identify a set of table cells as all being part of a group, such as those that indicate "wins" in a race.

You can use an id selector to identify one individual element and associate a CSS rule just for that element. For example, if you had an element whose id attribute had a value of "mainheadline", you could write a rule that only applies to that one element like this (note that the id selector begins with a # sign):

#mainheadline {font-weight:bold;}

Meanwhile the class selector will apply rules to any elements whose class attribute has a particular value. For example, if several elements had a class attribute whose value was "winner" then you could use a rule like this to indicate those elements should be written in a bold typeface (note that the class selector begins with a full stop):

.winner {font-weight:bold;}

Let's look at a complete example. Here is an HTML table with race winners' details. You can see the simple style sheet that is associated with the HTML page on the right, and the page that you would see in the browser beneath that.

You can use id and class selectors to match elements whose id or class attributes have specific values.

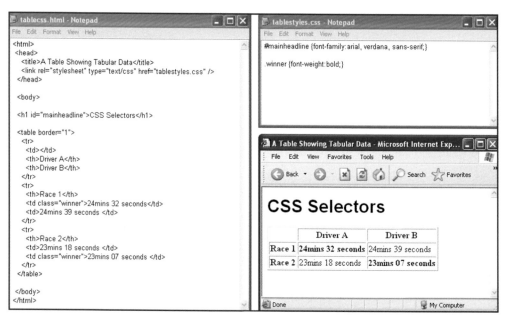

Now that we know how to write a style rule, the question is: what different properties can affect an element, and what possible values can these properties take? We don't have space to cover all the properties in CSS but we will look at some of the most common.

Font properties

If you want to change the typeface that some text is written in, then you can use the following properties. The most common use of these properties would be to specify a typeface you want the page to be written in and its size.

Property	Purpose	Examples
font-family	List of typefaces to be used, in order of preference. Usually this list should end with serif or sans-serif	font-family: Arial, Verdana, sans-serif;
font-size	Size of font, usually given in pixels (px) or points (pt)	font-size:12px; font-size:12pt;
font-weight	Should font be normal or bold typeface	font-weight: bold;
font-style	Should typeface be italic	font-style:italic;

You can also use a shorthand font property that allows you to specify any of these properties in one declaration. For example:

font: 12px bold italic arial, sans-serif;

Examples of controlling presentation of fonts.

You should be aware that designers tend to stick to some of the most common fonts, like Arial, Verdana, Times, Times New Roman, Courier and Helvetica, because a browser will only show the required font if it is installed on the machine. This is why you should specify lists of fonts in case your first choice is not available and cannot be displayed.

When professional designers work on a site, they usually select up to three fonts and stick to just using those. Mixing and matching lots of fonts on the same page tends to look quite amateurish.

Examples of controlling
presentation of text.

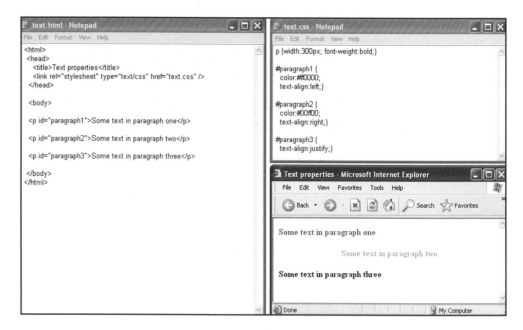

Text properties

Here are some properties that allow you to control the
appearance of text (beyond which typeface is used):

Property	Purpose	Examples
Color	Change the colour of the text used. Note the American English spelling. We explain how colours are written below	color:#ffffff; color:#000000; color:ff0000;
text-align	The alignment of text. Values are: left, center, right and justify Note the American English spelling again	text-align:right; text-align:justify;
vertical-align	The vertical alignment of text. Values are: top, middle, bottom	vertical-align:top; vertical-align: bottom;

The text-align and vertical-align properties are given in relation

to the containing element, so a paragraph might be left aligned
and a table heading might be centred.

Colours are specified using six-character hexadecimal codes
that describe the amount of red, green and blue required to make
that colour. 0 means none of that colour and f means the
maximum amount of that colour. Here are some examples:

Colour	Hexadecimal code
White	ffffff
Black	000000
Red	ff0000
Green	00ff00
Blue	0000ff

For an extensive reference with 216 different colours and their
codes, check out **www.visibone.com/colorlab**. This tool also
provides you with a handy reference that helps you choose
colours to complement your choices.

Visibone has a handy colour
picking tool.

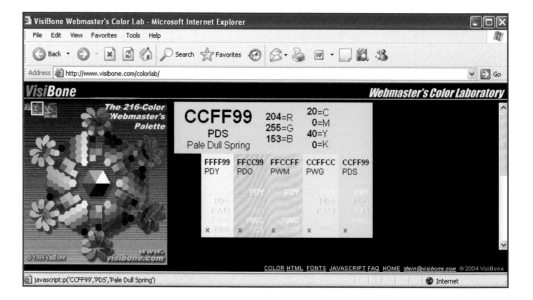

PART

Introducing the box model

When making your page look attractive using cascading style sheets, it really helps to understand that CSS treats every element as a box (this is known as the CSS box model). You can literally imagine an invisible box being created around every element that lives inside the <body> element of your HTML document.

There are two key types of boxes:

- **Block-level boxes** which are stacked on top of each other. Each new block level box looks like it is on a new line. For example, heading and paragraph elements always appear one above the other.
- **Inline boxes** which can be laid out next to each other without starting on a new line. Examples include the <i> and <b> elements. Obviously enough, you would not want one bold word in a paragraph to have to go on its own line.

Opposite you can see the box model in action, with a border around each box:

The importance of the box model becomes much clearer when you meet the next set of properties, which allow you to control borders, margins and padding.

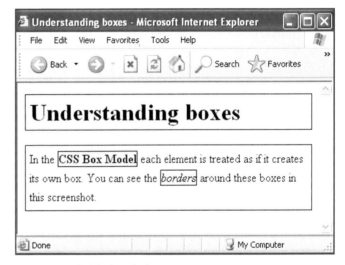

Each element inside the <body> of an HTML document creates an invisible box. Here you can see where the edges of the boxes would be if they were visible.

Borders, margins and padding

As we just explained, you can think of CSS treating each element as if it is in its own box. Each box has three properties: a border that is the edge of the box, a margin that is around the box, and padding that is between the border and the actual element content.

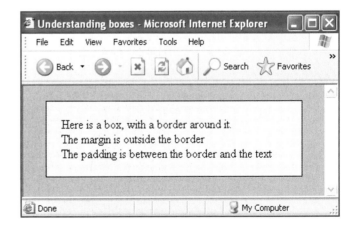

Each box has a border and can have a margin around it and padding inside it.

163

Border properties

By default the border of the box created by an element is invisible. However, you can control the border using these three properties:

Property	Purpose	Examples
border-width	The width of the border, which is usually specified in pixels (px)	border-width: 2px;
border-color	The colour of the border (note the American English spelling of colour). The value should be a hexadecimal colour value	border-color: #ff0000;
border-style	The style of the border. The most common values are solid, dotted and dashed	border-style: solid;

You can specify the border for each side of a box by using properties specific to that side:

border-top-width	border-top-color	border-top-style
border-right-width	border-right-color	border-right-style
border-bottom-width	border-bottom-color	border-bottom-style
border-left-width	border-left-color	border-left-style

You can also use a single shorthand border property, like this:

border: 3px solid #000000;

That gives us a 3-pixel wide solid black border.

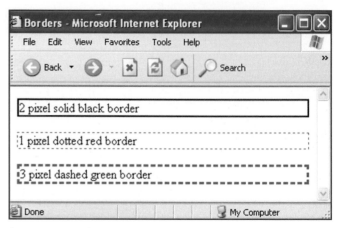

Some examples of borders.

Setting margins

You can set the margin *around* any box using the margin property. The size is usually specified in pixels. Margins are particularly helpful when you want to ensure that there is space between elements. For example, if you have text next to an image, then it is a good idea to have some space between the border of the image and the text. This looks professional and makes the text easier to read.

Setting padding

Padding is used when you need space *inside* a box, and is often measured in pixels. It is particularly useful in table cells to make sure that the content of the table cell does not meet the border of the table. This extra space makes it much easier to read the content of the table. For example, this rule indicates that all table cells should have 10 pixels of padding between the border and the content:

th, td {padding:10px;}

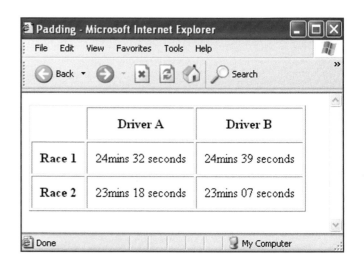

Adding padding to table cells makes them easier to read.

Colours of boxes

If you want to control the colour of a box, there are two very handy properties which carry hexadecimal code values (just like the ones we met in the section on font colours):

Property	Purpose	Examples
Color	Controls the foreground colour of a box	color:#ff0000;
Background-color	Controls the background colour of a box	background-color:#efefef;

It is important when choosing colours, and indeed when working on colour schemes for your site, to choose colours that work well together. Perhaps look at design books or other websites for inspiration. You could even look at colour charts that are available from DIY stores. When using combinations of foreground and background colours, you must ensure that there is sufficient contrast to enable to you read any text or see any pictures.

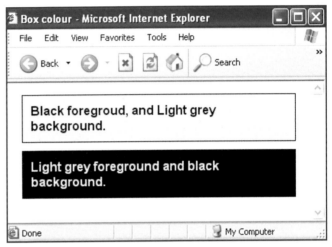

Changing colours of boxes.

Grouping elements using <div> and <span>

Having learned about creating CSS style sheets we should now backtrack and consider two final HTML elements which are particularly useful when working with CSS. Both of these elements are used to group together sets of related HTML elements. This is particularly helpful when you want to apply a style or set of styles to a group of elements. For example, the main links on a site might all use the same style and have a border around them in order to create a navigation bar.

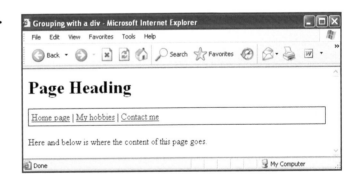

A <div> element is ideal for grouping together elements and applying the same styles to all of them.

- The <div> element creates a block level box, and can therefore be used with elements that create either block level boxes (such as the <p> and <h1> elements, which always start on a new line) and inline boxes (which can appear next to each other).
- The <span> element creates an inline box, and therefore can only be used with elements that create inline boxes (such as the <a>, <img /> and <b> elements).

By way of an example, here you can see a <div> element being used to create a navigation bar for a web page. It is used to create a containing block-level element around a set of <a> elements:

Creating your first site – using CSS

Having learned how CSS is applied to an HTML document, we should now revisit the example personal site that we built at the end of the section on HTML and transform it using CSS.

Add a link element into the head of the HTML documents so that these documents are associated with the correct stylesheet (mysite.css). It is a good idea to do this before writing the stylesheet so that you can test the stylesheet as you get to work on the HTML document.

Open a new document in your text editor for the style sheet. Save this file as mysite.css in the same folder as your HTML pages. Then open up the HTML file in a browser next to the CSS style sheet. To see the effect of the changes as you make them, save the CSS file and then reload the page in the browser (Ctrl+R).

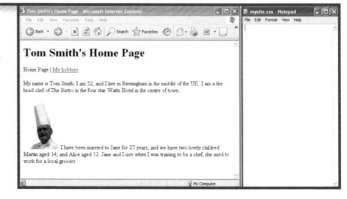

To start with, we will add a rule with some properties to control the appearance of the whole of the page. In order for the properties to apply to the whole document, the selector will indicate the body element.

Inside this rule, we will add properties to control the colour of the text with the color property and the background colour of the page with the background-color property. We will make the text dark grey using a value of #333333; and a background colour of very light grey using a value of #d6d6d6. We will also ensure that all text in the document appears in one of our preferred typefaces using the font-family property. The first preference of font will be Arial.

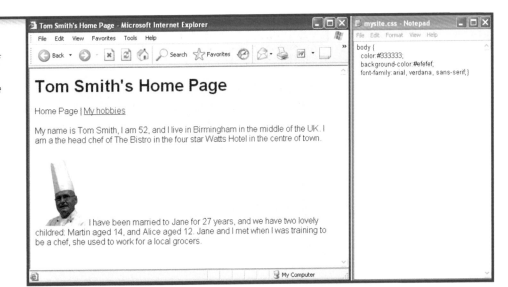

Next let's give the level 1 heading a black background and use white text to make it really stand out from the rest of the page. To do this we need to add an h1 selector to the style sheet, and add a color property with a value of #ffffff (white) and a background-color property with a value of #000000 (black).

When there is a visible border to a box, as with the h1 element, it is nice to add padding to create a gap between the edge of the box and the content of the box (in this case, the text).

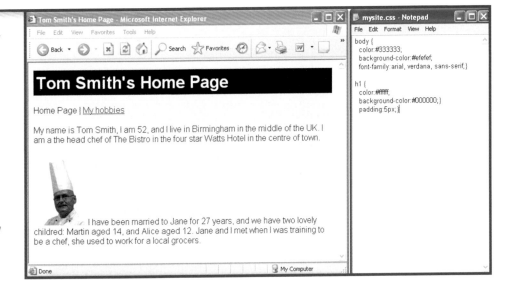

In order to control the presentation of the navigation items, we need to add a class attribute to the <p> element in the HTML document. This can be used to distinguish this <p> element from other <p> elements. The class attribute should have a value of "navigation" to indicate that this paragraph of text represents the navigation for the document.

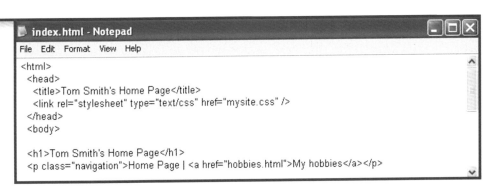

Now that we can uniquely identify the <p> element that acts as navigation, we can use a class selector to apply rules to it. We can set the color of the text to be a light grey using the color property, and the background colour to be red using the background-color property. In order for the background colour of the paragraph to spread across the width of the page, like the background colour of the heading element, you need to add a width attribute with a value of 100%.

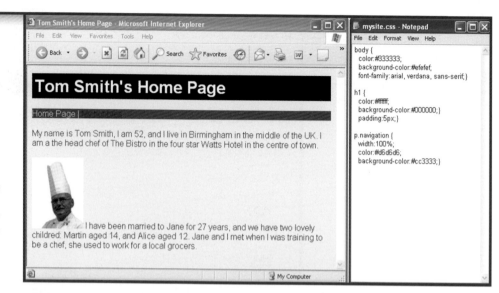

To make the navigation slightly easier to read, we should make it bold using the font-weight property. We can also add padding to create some space between the text and the edges of the red box.

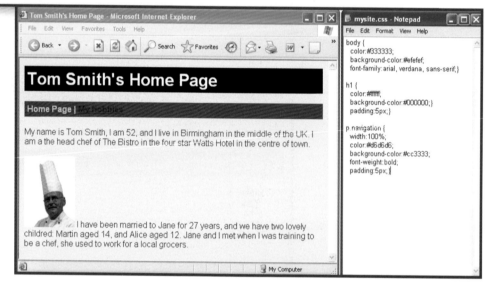

To make the link in the navigation fit in a little better with the rest of the page, let's make the text for the link white (rather than the default blue that most browsers use to show links). We just want this rule to apply to links in this navigation bar, so we have to write a slightly more complex selector in the rule, indicating that this rule should only apply to <a> elements that are children of the <p> element whose class attribute has a value of navigation. We have already seen how to select this paragraph using a class selector, and to indicate that we just want <a> elements within this element, we leave a space followed by the name of this element:
p.navigation a {}

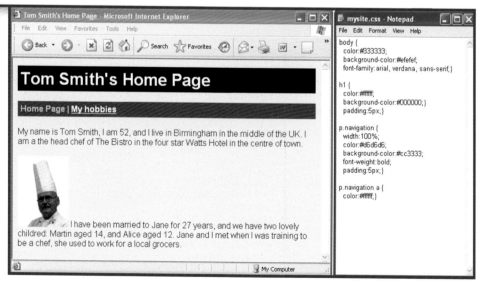

Let's add a border around the photo with the border property. We can set the width, style and the colour of the line with just one border property. We should also add a margin around the edge of the photo to prevent the text touching it. This makes the page look better and also easier to read.

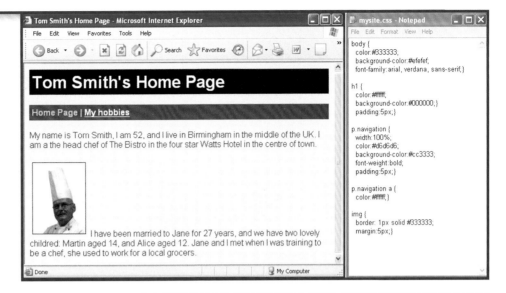

There is a gap between the <h1> element and the navigation which it would be nice to remove (bringing these two elements together). In order to do this we need the margin element. If you remember back to the description of the box model, a margin is placed around each box, and by default browsers add a margin around both heading and paragraph elements. In order to remove this margin, we should give the margin property on these two elements a value of 0px.

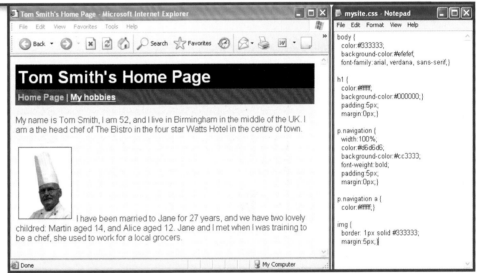

Finally, we are going to look at one last property that we have not discussed yet. In order to push the image in the second paragraph of the page across to the right-hand side of the screen, we can add the float property to the properties in the rule that applies to the <img /> element. This float property will have a value of right. While we are at it, we also need to set a width for this "floating" element, as otherwise it will take up the full width of the page. Add a width property with a value of 100px. Done. This simple page now looks a whole lot more attractive, courtesy of a style sheet.

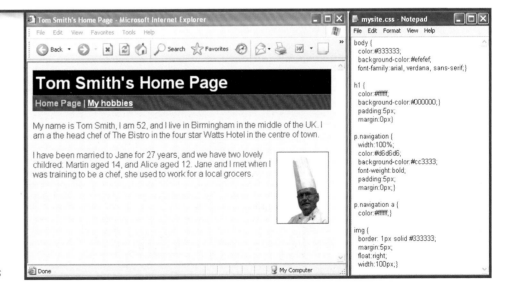

BUILD YOUR OWN WEBSITE

PART ⑦ Appendices

PART

Appendix 1 – Search engine optimisation

When you've gone to the trouble of setting up a website you want as many people as possible to visit it, but how do you let them know you're there? Apart from the many incidental ways you can promote your site such as getting it listed in relevant print publications, adding it to your business cards and letterheads, and getting it listed in print and online directories, there are two far more effective methods of attracting visitors:

- Get as many sites a possible to display a link to yours.
- Make sure that your site can be found easily by internet search engines such as Google.

Of the two, the second is by far the most important. Figures suggest that at least 80% of website visitors arrive from a search engine.

How search engines work

If you're going to tweak your website to make it highly visible to internet search engines, you need to know how search engines work. Basically they have three components: a spider (also known as a crawler), a database and an enquiry system. The spider is a program that roams the web examining as many sites as possible. When it visits a site it also follows all the links it finds (these might be to other pages on the same site or to external sites run by other people). The information it finds is stored in the database and indexed. Once a spider thinks it has visited all the sites it can find, it starts all over again looking for changes.

The Yahoo and Google directories are not search engines, they are human-edited and thematically-linked indexes to useful sites. To get your site in the Yahoo directory you pay a fee, but the Google directory is part of the free Open Directory Project and you may suggest your own site for inclusion by visiting **http://dmoz.org/add.html**.

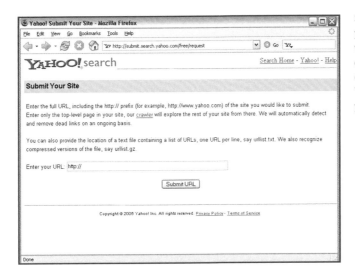

Search engine spiders should find your site for themselves, but if you want to make absolutely sure you can submit URLs manually to each search engine. To submit to Yahoo visit **http://submit.search. yahoo.com/free/request**.

When a user types a phrase into a search engine's enquiry system (which is the only part of a search engine users ever actually see), the phrase is checked not against actual websites but against the indexed database. That's why searches are so fast. It's rather like looking up "plumbers" in *Yellow Pages* instead of reading through the entire book until you get to the page with plumbers on it, which would take weeks.

When a search engine has matched a user's query against its database, it lists the sites it has found in what it considers to be the most significant order: in other words, with the best matches listed first. Search engines often find many thousands of sites matching a particular query so it's crucial that yours should be placed high on the list and preferably on the first page of results. Ideally it will be at the top, but that can be a difficult trick to pull off.

What search engines look for

Every search engine has its own algorithms. Algorithms in this sense are sets of rules that search engines use to decide what's important and what's not. Unfortunately these algorithms are guarded as closely as the secret recipes for Coca Cola or Kentucky Fried Chicken, because the search engine companies know that web designers would use tricks to artificially boost the rankings of their sites if they knew the exact algorithms. But what is absolutely certain, and what is common to all search engines, is that two elements of a site are of overriding importance when deciding rankings: keywords and links.

Each search engine decides for itself which phrases are keywords based on factors such as how close it is to the top of the page, whether it appears in the title, whether it is used as a link and whether you have specifically specified it as a keyword. With a little planning and imagination you can "seed" your web page with phrases that will almost certainly be picked up by most search engines as keywords. The trick is to make sure these keywords are as close as possible to what most users will key into a search engine when they're looking for sites like yours.

To increase the chances of keywords being recognised as such, you should repeat them several times in the body text of each page. Search engines also take account of something called keyword density, which means they look for a high ratio of keywords to ordinary text. Experts reckon that keyword density should be somewhere between 3% and 8% (let's call it 5%), which means that EACH of your keywords should be used 5 times for every hundred words. Bear in mind that search engines concentrate on nouns, verbs and other significant words and do not count so-called stop words which are articles, pronouns, prepositions and other parts of speech.

All the web search engines are in competition for the same users and they're all trying to provide a top-notch service, which means presenting users with sites genuinely relevant to their searches and not directing them to revenue-chasing sites that are padded out with spurious keywords but no real content. Such sites are classified as web spam (as opposed to the more familiar email spam) and they're ignored by search engines. Be sure to play fair with keywords or you could find yourself branded as a web spammer and have your site sidelined or ignored.

Visit the FAQ pages of Google and other major search engines to find out how they analyse web pages, then plan your own site accordingly.

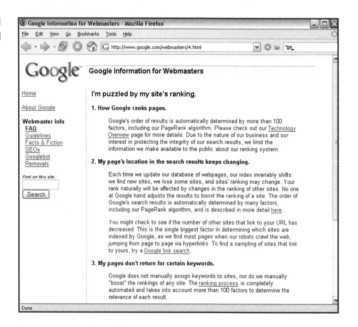

For a list of most of over 500 common stop words visit **www.searchengineworld.com/spy/ stopwords.htm**.

Meta tags and links

Meta tags are special HTML identifying tags that appear in the header section of every web page. The tags' contents don't display on the page but they can be seen by search engines, and although there are quite a few different types the two most important ones are the meta description and meta keywords tags. If you decide to include them (you don't have to), you should place a complete and glowing description of your page after the meta description tag and a list of keywords after the meta keywords tag. Sadly, because these two tags have been so misused in the past by people filling them with screeds of irrelevant and misleading information, most search engines now ignore them. Google doesn't pay attention to either tag, but some rival search engines use one or the other so it's worth including meta tags if you want to cover all the bases.

The way your site uses links is of far more importance to a search engine than whether you've used meta tags. Links between the pages of your site are the way a spider finds its way from the home page to the really meaty parts. Without a well-planned system of internal links, only a fraction of your site might get indexed. Just as important are the links made to your site from external sites. If a large number of sites link to yours, then your site will be regarded as an important one and will be given a better ranking, but not all links are equal: search engines confer a higher ranking on your site if the other sites that link to it are themselves highly ranked. Search engine spiders track links back to their sources and only regard a site as being relevant to yours if it is thematically related and uses similar keywords. If the links all come from the personal websites of friends and family they won't make much impact on your site's status.

You can find relevant sites to link to by typing your site's main keywords into a search engine. You'll discover sites that might be usefully linked to yours and you can then approach them with requests to exchange links. If your site is tailored for e-commerce this is also a way of identifying your competitors. You can't expect competitors to be interested in exchanging links, but once you know who they are you can find out who is linking to their sites, and then ask the same sites to link to yours.

Need more help?

Type "search engine optimisation" into any search engine and you'll find thousands of sites trying to sell you software, books, site design services and marketing tools, but some of the sites do contain genuinely useful free advice, information and interactive resources. One of the best is the webmasters section at Search Engine Watch. Go directly to it by typing **http://searchenginewatch.com/webmasters**. Also worth a look is **www.1hour-search-engine-optimisation.com**, which features a ten-part guide to getting better rankings on search engines. This is extracted from Michael Wong's best-selling e-book on the subject. If it's software you're after, try WebPosition Gold from **www.web-positiongold.com**. The standard version costs $149 so it's not cheap, but there's a 30-day trial version you can play around with.

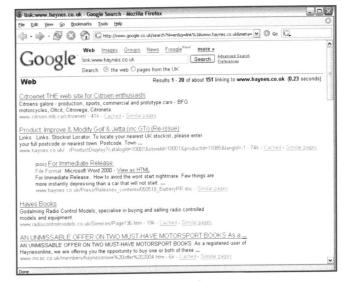

To learn how many sites link to your site (or any other) simply type link:sitename into Google. There must be no space between the colon and the site's URL, which in this example is **www.haynes.co.uk**.

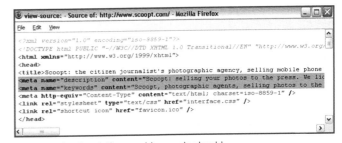

Meta tags for descriptions and keywords should be placed between the <head> and </head> tags at the top of each web page (see p.129).

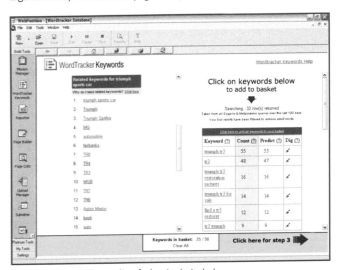

WebPosition Gold is a suite of nine tools to help with search engine optimisation. This screen shows the keyword analysis tool, which not only suggests new keywords but also reports which sites are already using them.

Tips and tricks

The top tip for pushing your site onto the first page of search engines is to get a domain name that embodies your most significant keywords. If all the suitable domains have gone, then put each page in a folder whose name includes suitable keywords. You can see how effective this is if you type "lavender products" into your favourite search engine. When we tried it, eight of the top ten sites listed by Google contained one or both words in their URLs.

● Pick keywords that contain other keywords. For example, if your main business is selling garden tools, use "gardening tools" as one of your key phrases. Search engines can understand compound words so you'll get hits from people searching for both "garden" and "gardening".

● Place the most important keywords in the HTML title tag of every page, and repeat them in the body text close to the top of the page.

● Place keywords in the order users are most likely to type them. Search engines will then judge your page more relevant than others with the same words in random order.

● Use different keywords for each page to reflect the actual content.

● Don't use blocks of graphical text unless there is no alternative. Not only do they slow up the page for people on dial-up connections, but they can't be indexed by search engines. Stick to HTML text wherever possible, and if you must use graphics attach an ALT text description to each one.

● Include as many links as possible (using HTML text not graphics) between the pages on your site. Put them inside the body text and/or at the bottom of each page where both humans and search engines will be able to find them easily.

● Don't attempt to fool search engines by repeating the same keywords hundreds of times, and concealing them by making their text colour the same as the background colour. This is an old trick that every search engine now recognises, and it might lead to the page being rejected as web spam.

● Don't join a link farm, which is an exchange system where hundreds of unrelated sites are cross-linked to each other through pages full of nothing but links. People do this hoping to boost the apparent popularity of their sites but most search engines will see through the ruse and completely ignore the participating sites.

Appendix 2 – Building an online shop

From sole traders to giant corporations, companies big and small have discovered that the internet is a great way to find new customers – but you don't need to be Tesco to build an online shop. In this section, we discover the different ways you can sell things online.

Shops that never close

Some of the best-known e-commerce companies can also be found in high streets and shopping centres. Tesco is a typical example: it uses the web not only to promote its stores but also as part of a home-delivery operation and as a means of selling specialist items such as wine and financial services at discount prices. In contrast, a great many other companies exist only on the web and depend on it for their survival and business growth.

Firms such as Dabs.com were quick to realise the potential of selling online. The site has won a shelf-full of awards and processes more than 5000 orders per day.

Absolutely anything legal (and some things that aren't) can be purchased on the web.

Of these, Amazon is probably the biggest and best known. Even if you've never bought a book or CD from Amazon yourself, the chances are you know somebody who has.

Whether you're interested in setting up a web presence for an existing business or creating an online enterprise from scratch, don't let the technical details put you off: it has never been easier to set up an e-commerce site. Just be sure that before you take the plunge and put up a live site, you've already sorted out the "back-end" of the business, including having sufficient stock to meet demand, plus a well-organised packaging and delivery operation.

Web shop essentials

Established companies use networked computers to perform administrative and financial functions. Part of the arrangement is usually a structured database system storing details of goods, prices, suppliers and the current stock situation. To add web sales to a system like this is no simple matter. Typically, you need specialist software to link the network to a dedicated internet server, and expert help will be required to implement and maintain both hardware and software. The result will be a fully integrated system that not only provides an internet shop window for the company's products but also passes details of web transactions to the existing order system for processing.

At the other extreme, you can set up a new small enterprise using a rented web shop to sell your goods. Whenever an item is sold, you're informed by email and it's up to you to process the order in any way you see fit. There is no connection between the web shop and your own PC or network. In theory, you could even run this type of business without a PC by using a mobile phone to receive email notifications.

In between the two extremes are dozens of web trading systems involving varying degrees of complexity, but what they all have in common is the identical experience they provide to customers. Potential buyers are able to search or browse for products of interest, and having found a product they can store it in a temporary electronic "basket" while they continue to shop. There is a checkout system where purchases are totalled and carriage charges are added, and there are forms for the collection of personal information such as names and delivery addresses. Finally, of course, there must be a secure means of accepting electronic payments by credit or debit card.

Impulse purchases and last-minute gifts are the stock-in-trade of many web stores.

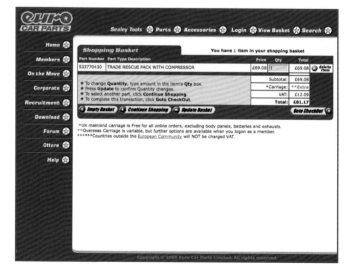

Whether it's called a shopping basket or shopping cart, it's where goods are held until a customer is ready to check out and pay.

The simplest solution

For start-up businesses with no pre-existing company website, the simplest and cheapest way of getting into e-commerce is to rent an e-shop that can be configured and set up using only a web browser. The resulting web pages do not reside on your computer at all, but on the computers of the company renting you the shop. When sales are made and payment has been received (usually through PayPal or WorldPay), you receive a notification by email. The cost of renting a web shop varies according to a number of factors, but principally it's the number of different products you wish to sell, the amount of web space you'll need and the level of traffic you expect to handle. Charges range from £10 to £60 a month. At the lower end of the scale you may be restricted to selling only a handful of products, while at the upper end you're allowed hundreds of products and will be able to set up a searchable product catalogue complete with photographs and descriptions.

One of the disadvantages of a web shop maintained solely through a web browser is that you don't get a chance to customise your site other than in ways provided by the host. This makes it difficult to give your shop site a unique look and feel, and it means you have no base for further development if you decide you've outgrown your existing site. On the other hand you can operate your site from literally any computer with an internet connection.

More advanced web shops

A step up from the simplest browser-driven web shop is one where you construct your site with the help of design templates and software wizards. The finished shop is translated into HTML code, which you are allowed to modify to a certain extent by changing elements such as headers and footers, and by adding scripts. A script is a fragment of code you can paste into the HTML at specific points to customise various elements. You pay a monthly rental which covers the shop's design tools and the cost of hosting it on a fast internet server. Financial transactions are usually limited to PayPal, but sites like these can easily be upgraded if your business grows.

Most shop hosts offer a tiered pricing system where for a small extra payment you can sell more products and use more pictures on your site, and you'll be given greater freedom to add personal touches. If you pay the very top rate, you'll get a web shop that can be fully customised and completely integrated with your company's main website. Other benefits include being able to download transactions and customer data in a form suitable for using with your database or spreadsheet program, and there is no restriction on the number of products in your catalogue. You might also be covered by a shared secure site certificate enabling you to accept confidential information such as credit card numbers from your customers. Most web shop providers (regardless of the service level chosen) are able to provide comprehensive site traffic reports and help with getting your shop listed on internet search engines.

A fully-functional website constructed and maintained using only a web browser, available from **www.doyourownsite.co.uk**.

At 1&1 Internet (**www.1and1.co.uk**) you can buy almost any internet service, including upgradeable web shops.

The bespoke option

Hand-made e-commerce sites come in all shapes and sizes. If you're already running a successful website and you understand the basics of HTML coding you can graft a simple shopping cart system onto your existing site and this will enable you to take customer orders and link to PayPal for payment processing. It won't cost you anything to implement and there'll be no monthly charges other than what you're already paying for web hosting.

Although bespoke sites are a cheap option for those with the ability to create their own, serious business users are not drawn to them for this reason. For them, site design is usually sub-contracted to a professional designer who will produce an eye-catching site that works as it should and is fully secure. Larger organisations might even employ a full-time web wizard, and host their e-commerce facility on the company's own server instead of through a hosting service, especially if e-commerce transactions are to be linked to the company's existing order processing system.

The advantages of a bespoke site are that you can:

- seamlessly integrate your company's e-commerce and offline trading operations;
- set-up an e-commerce site that accurately reflects your company's corporate identity;
- customise the contents of your site for different countries and currencies;
- enjoy total flexibility to offer the services you think your customers need, rather than the ones built into a web shop template;
- process payments from virtually any source.

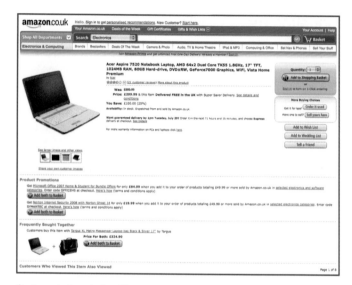

Custom-designed sites like Amazon's can generate extra trade by making recommendations based on past purchases.

When selling essentials, the simplest approach is sometimes the best: make it easy for customers to find exactly what they want and they'll come back time and again.

Handling money online

E-commerce could not exist without safe ways of making payments online. There are several ways of going about this and the method that's right for you will depend on the nature and volume of your business, and on whether you already have a merchant account with your bank that allows you to take credit cards.

If you don't have such an account, perhaps because you are just starting up, the simplest and most convenient systems are those run by payment bureaux such Nochex (**www.nochex.com**), PayPal (**www.paypal.com**) and WorldPay (**www.worldpay.com**). Once you've established an account with one of these companies, you will be provided with the necessary software to link your e-commerce system to the payment bureau's own site. When your customers check out the contents of their shopping baskets on your site they are transferred to the payment bureau's site where they enter their credit or debit card details. Once payment has been received, you are notified by the payment bureau and can then process the sale. Almost anybody can open a service bureau account provided they have a current bank account and a credit card. Charges are generally calculated per transaction and may be as high as 4.5%. Though this seems steep, there are no set-up costs and no subscriptions or service fees to pay, so if you make no sales in a particular period you pay no fees. This makes a payment bureau the ideal system for start-up and micro businesses, which is why many of the entry-level web shops incorporate them as the only option for processing online payments.

Established businesses with merchant accounts at their banks and who are already equipped with a swipe machine for point-of-sale credit card transactions can upgrade their merchant account to accept "customer not present" transactions. This allows customers to phone, fax or send their credit card details for manual processing, but its too labour-intensive if you anticipate handling a significant volume of online sales. It's far better to ask your bank if it will add Internet Merchant Services (IMS) to your merchant account. If it will, the only other thing you need is a Payment Service Provider (PSP) to handle individual transactions on your behalf. In effect, a PSP acts in place of a swipe machine by collecting customer details over the internet and passing them to your bank for authorisation.

Although it sounds complicated and expensive to operate an e-commerce site using a merchant account, it can actually work out cheaper despite having to pay set-up, fixed charges and commissions to both your bank and your PSP. It all depends on whether you expect to maintain a sufficiently high volume of transactions. Another benefit is that banks perform stringent checks before authorising a customer for IMS, so the very fact you're not using a payment bureau gives your business instant credibility.

SVP sells optical discs and related items through its website at **http://svp.co.uk**. Its thousands of satisfied customers all pay their bills through payment bureaux including PayPal and Google Checkout.

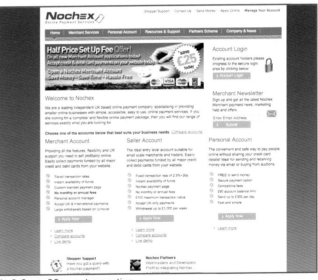

At 2.6p + 20p per transaction, Nochex is probably the cheapest way to handle payments up to £100, but PayPal and WorldPay are better for larger amounts and international transactions.

Index